Bush Pilots' Wives

LeNora Conkle

Publication Consultants

PO Box 221974 Anchorage, Alaska 99522-1974

ISBN 1-888125-77-2

Library of Congress Catalog Card Number: 00-108757

Other Books by LeNora Conkle

Trail of the Eagle

Wind on the Water

Hunting the Way it Was

Manufactured in the United States of America.

Dedication

Dedicated to the bush pilots' wives.

For the men there was the lure of adventure that brought them to Alaska; a camaraderie of hunting interests, and for some it was the opportunity to own land and/or work for generous wages. We now know the colorful history of those early settlers in Alaska, such are the stories of men and their adventures in the gold mines, big game hunting and pioneering trails in the skies over this vast land. Yet the women were a part of those days also. Women worked alongside their men and endured the same hardships. They laughed, loved and gave birth to new generations. Some were of an era in Alaska when those early bush pilots were making legends. A limited few were pilots and big game guides and made legends of their own.

The women who stayed with their men were a special breed of gals. They could handle their own share of the work, the problems, the kids, make important decisions on short notice as well as the accidents and emergencies which were sure to happen when hubby was away flying. Babies were noted for arriving when daddy was gone from home making a living. Wives were a working partner and called on to help in a variety of situations. They had all the qualities of those sturdy women, as well as the men, who have made Alaska what it is today. Just as it has been down through the ages. Countless women at home doing what has to be done when the men are gone to war or to other places men go to provide for the family at home.

Table of Contents

Acknowledgments

To my son Glen Huntley for his dedicated time at the computer helping and encouraging me to get this manuscript finished and his patience with my total computer illiteracy, when time after time, he had much of my pages to do over. For his correcting, editing, and trying to teach me what I seemed to be doing wrong instead of remembering how it should be done. Without his constant help I would have gone back to my obsolete typewriter.

To the bush pilots' wives I have included here, who were willing to share their stories and get them to me, and not lose patience with the many phone calls, and questionnaires sent to them. There were many more wives I would have been pleased to include their stories, had they wished to participate.

These wives, as well as myself, are only an example of what the majority of the professional bush pilots' expected of her. These are only a portion of the stories these wives could have told. To all our pilot husbands who had confidence in our ability to handle whatever situations each day brought.

Also, to both the fathers, and mothers, of all these children who included their children in all aspects of their work, who taught their kids responsibility at a very early age. These children now have children of their own. Every one of them are a credit to their parents and grandparents, as well as respected citizens in their communities and society.

Especially to my publisher, Evan Swensen, for his patience and help.

Introduction

What about those wives and the kids who were home waiting for the familiar sound of the returning airplane. But instead of the husband and father, it was a friend or an official who brought the dreaded news—he had crashed or was missing! Some of those familiar names; Jules Thibedeau—known as the "Walking Pilot" because he had walked back from many crash landing. Walter "Walk-Away Wally" Rochester also a "walking pilot," always walked in before he was reported missing—right up to his last crash.

Kenneth "Ken" Bunch—a noted pilot who had always managed to return with the airplane he flew until that fatal day when everyone involved thought it was weather that held him from returning.

There are many books published about Alaska bush pilots but seldom is anything mentioned about the wife and children. Now and then there will be mentioned about one or another of those early-day pilots being stationed in a remote village, Nome or Bettles or some such place where he is always on call for emergencies besides the regular schedules, he even moves the family there. The wife is never mentioned for her ability to cope with what ever types of inconveniences she is left to cope with. Raising the kids without indoor plumbing and the modern conveniences she has been used to, is a hassle in itself without the additional emergencies that always happens.

Chapter One

Pioneering Adventures

Alaska conjures up exciting pictures of adventure of many varieties. Jack London and James Olive Curwood books were access to dreams and an escape from a mundane life in a small town in Idaho where nothing of importance ever happens. That was my point of view, of course, when I was still in grade school.

I vividly remember a barnstorming pilot putting on a mind-boggling show in the skies over the open hay and potato fields near Hazelton, Idaho. A few of the bravest men who could spare five dollars for a ride took a short flight. The name of that pilot didn't register and stay in my young mind but the desire to know a man who could do such brave things as this young pilot was doing did stay. As airplanes grew more common over the years I never forgot that vicariously of course ride in his airplane. It was a second hand Curtis JN (Jenny), or it might have been a Curtis Robin. From that time on the pilots who flew them held my interest.

It was a long road with many experiences before I made Alaska my home. My new home in Alaska with a husband who had plans for his future in Alaska when the war was over. I met C.M. "Bud" Conkle when he was stationed at the U.S. Marine Corps Base in San Diego, California. I was living in San Diego at that time and operating my own business. We met soon after graduating from Boot Camp, before he was sent overseas.

On our first date, Alaska, the new frontier and the opportunities it offered, was all we talked about. We had a mutual interest. He talked of his plans to learn to fly an airplane and to be a big game guide and a bush pilot, in the Territory of Alaska.

I expressed my desire to be a pilot too if the opportunity ever presented itself. On a second date when "Conk," as his Marine Buddies nicknamed him, brought me a book to read "WE LIVE IN ALASKA" by Bud & Connie Helmerick. Reading that book had me giving a lot of thought to pulling up stakes and going. This cowboy type from the Jemez Mountains in New Mexico definitely had my attention. I was very much impressed by his patriotic attitude as well as the jaunty way he wore his Marine cap and uniform. He had enlisted in the Marines just before Pearl Harbor in WW II.

Bud and LeNora Before he headed over seas in World War II.

C.M. "Bud" Conkle knew what he wanted for his future and he didn't let too many things stand in his way. He had found a friend with a mutual interest in Alaska but this gal wasn't making any promises because of the way the war was going in those early years, there wasn't much of a chance he'd be returning. Few Marines did. The ship he was on after leaving Okinawa was on its way to Japan but before they arrived the Japanese surrendered, so the Marine unit of the Second Engineer Division were the occupation forces instead of facing a bloody battle few Marines would have survived. This Marine did return and he was still going to Alaska and I was going with him—so he told me. Gee! I don't remember saying yes, but I'm sure I didn't say no!

Clement "Bud" Conkle received his honorable discharge papers from the Marine Corps base in San Diego mid-January and we were married in April in San Diego. Our honeymoon was the six weeks traveling from California to Fairbanks, Alaska in May & June 1946. We bought one of the first two civilian Willeys Jeeps that arrived in San Diego and with a second hand trailer (with poor tires for the load we packed on it). We

The log house we built at Eagle Trail Ranch.

bid friends good bye and were on our way to Alaska. I was soon to realize just how determined this husband of mine was to achieve his goals.

In 1946 the Alaska-Canadian (Alcan) Highway starting from Dawson Creek in Canada to Delta Junction in Alaska was still considered a military highway and not open to civilian traffic. Travel was not encouraged on it, and anyone wishing to travel on the Alcan to Alaska would be required to get written permission from a designated office in Seattle, Washington or permission from Ed-

monton Canada. Our inquiry at the Seattle office was discourag-
ing. "Best wait until next year and there will be a good chance it
will be open." Other than that no one in that office seemed to
know anything about the condition of the Alcan Highway.

"No way are we going to wait a year!!" Bud emphatically
stated. "We could fly up there but can't get a satisfactory answer
as to when our Jeep and trailer would be shipped so we are on
our way to Edmonton. We'll take the chance we can drive on
the Alcan to Alaska."

"What if we drive all the way to Edmonton and are refused
permission? You were told it was best to write for permission
before driving there?" I thought it a logical question. "We'll go if
we have to make our own road," was his not so logical answer.
We had seven days of travel and overnight camping before
arriving at the Canadian Government office where we'd soon
know the answer to the question that had worried us those
many days. We had enjoyed those days of travel, beautiful scenery
and camps by exciting fishing streams, talking to many travelers
we met along our way, and relieved that we didn't meet any
who had been refused permission to travel the Alcan to Alaska
and we had met a few who like us, were on their way. One
disappointment encountered was the newly painted green Jeep
like ours that passed and honked but kept on going. It was
loaded like we were, with gas cans (Jerry-cans as they are called)
strapped to the sides, a sign on the back of the trailer they were
pulling read "ALASKA BOUND." We would have enjoyed talking to them but had a real surprise on meeting them in Fairbanks. He was the "Iceman." He had a job delivering ice to a
variety of homes in Fairbanks even in the winter months.

Chapter Two

Alaska Bound

We were at the Canadian government office in Edmonton, Canada, on a Monday morning before the doors were open. We didn't have long to wait and not as much red tape as we expected. They just asked if we had enough money and equipment to take care of ourselves all the way through Canada. The officer wasn't happy that we hadn't written for permission before driving all the way to Edmonton and didn't appear happy about the excuse Bud gave him. Reluctantly he gave us a permit to go on to Dawson Creek where the Alcan starts but told us that we could be turned back there. So, more days of worrying about will we get to go on, or will we have to turn around and go back!

I didn't hear all the conversation that went on in the of office at Dawson Creek, but Bud Conkle won the final argument and came out holding the permit and said, "We are on our way." That stern officer was all business and really chewed me out, but he finally gave in with a comment I didn't expect.

"You Americans built the highway so why should the Canadians keep you from using it," he said, and added, "I sure wish you a pleasant trip. Be sure to report in at the Canadian Customs on arrival at the Alaska border fourteen days from today. You look better equipped than some who are on their way. You'll surely meet up with a truck that went through here about two days ago, hauling a cow, a couple of dogs, and a few kids. I'll bet they will have a story to tell when they reach their destination in Alaska." We met them in Whitehorse, and they sure were a conversation piece with that cow. All the kids in town showed up at milking time. They couldn't believe that was where their milk came from.

Traveling on dusty, narrow, gravel roads with dust seeping into everything we had with us did not make the trip any more enjoyable. We made our overnight camps by quiet streams, away from the highway noises. Always with a good fishing stream, we never tired of fresh trout. I had left a modern home and a business I loved and had very limited camping experience. Bud was a very efficient person with many years of experiences behind him. He would have a cheery campfire going beside the clear bubbling steam and our tent set up with no help from me. I was too busy shaking the dust from everything he would be using, from the cooking utensils to dishes. To help I would peel the potatoes he was planning to cook in a fry pan over hot coals. I was a good observer to the way he cooked a steak or the fresh caught fish.

Our jeep had four new tires and two spares but the trailer had poor tires to start with and Bud did a lot of tire patching on patches. So soon after the war there just wasn't any new tires on the market. Bud spotted a trailer in a farmer's yard and stopped and talked him out of all four of those tires. Bud was indeed in luck that day because I wasn't about to abandon my sewing machine or any other of my "goodies" on that overloaded trailer. Without those tires it was looking like we'd have to abandon the trailer.

As we traveled farther on the Alcan what knowledge Bud and I lacked was the experience needed to know what to do about the over abundance of the blood thirsty mosquitoes we'd encounter should we make camp in a swampy area with no wind to slow them down. This was June and the new hatch was out and those vicious, buzzing little devils main interest was blood and our blood was on their menu. They tried to eat us alive. We had to keep a towel or leafy branch in one hand busy brushing them off while rushing a hasty dinner then retreat to the mosquito proof tent for the night or do without an awful lot of blood. With his tough hide Bud could tolerate more bites that I could. Eventually we did learn to camp where a strong breeze slowed them down but they didn't discourage easy.

At a camp ground while still in Canada we encountered some of the biggest and fiercest of those thirsty devils and our smudge fire wasn't slowing them in their dive-bombing efforts. A friendly stranger, a man traveling alone and on his way back to Alaska had a cherry bit of information he was happy to share, "You ain't seen nothing yet. These guys are pikers in comparison to Alaska mosquitoes. Thanks for that good news. I'll practice on them with my Colt Woodsman pistol" I said.

Those buzzing hoards plagued us in every camp site and if they could possibly be bigger and more of them in Alaska I was beginning to wonder about living there, but I'd still go and see how others tolerated them. I was soon to learn Bud's theory; "If some one else could do it he could too."

We were in our first camp in Alaska when some friendly Alaskans stopped to chat and gave us a bottle of 6-12 mosquito repellent the U.S. Army was furnishing for the solders. It was new and really worked, and it was indeed a blessed relief.

The further north we drove after leaving Dawson Creek the longer the days were and we were camping at night in almost broad daylight. Every day brought new sights as well as wild animals. Black bears and grizzlies were often seen along the highway as well as moose and smaller animals. It was exciting to see bands of wild sheep high in the mountains. All the more exciting to know we'd be making our home in a country where all those animals and more varieties would be our neighbors. Yes, even I, a gal from the city, was looking forward to living where they roamed in the wilds. A large gray wolf sauntered across the highway ahead of us and added to a day of beautiful mountain scenery. As much as I enjoyed each day's travel, I'll admit there were times when the dust from the road, smoke from camp fires, sweat from expended energy, and a quick bath in a cold stream, gave me a homesick feeling to stay overnight in a motel on nearing a town where there was one. His answer to my suggestion as how nice it would be to take a hot shower, wash our clothes and sleep in a night between sheets. "What's so tough about taking a bath and washing clothes in a river like the Indian women do? There's no shortage of rivers with good clean running water!" he answered, then went on with his logical explanation that it would be unwise to leave all our worldly possessions with the jeep and trailer when there was no way of locking them up. "What if we returned in the morning to find it all cleaned out, would we have the finances to replace it all in Alaska?"

"Gee thanks, my dear hubby," I'd glumly answer as he was

setting up camp so far out of a town or village it was no use of my being unreasonable. What I had wanted to say was; "What an introduction to a new bride to—roughing it.

Many times we camped and waited where bridges or roads were washed out or under construction or being repaired, all too often a two or three days wait. We'd set up our camp by a clear running stream that furnished us with fresh caught fish, now and then a nice fat duck to supplement our diet. We'd hike into interesting areas or climb a mountain those days. We had other delays too like when the trailer tongue broke and with improvised repairs we managed to limp into a town close by both times to get it welded. The road would be a muddy mess with deep ruts when it rained hard for more than one day at a time. Bud was a careful driver but the size of the rocks put on the road when it was being repaired were big and sharp and just no way of avoiding them all. Bud's vocabulary doesn't lack for colorful words, but on hearing a second new Jeep tire blow out he began to chant some of the most striking blaspheme I have ever heard but it was delivered with finesse.

We browsed in a store or around town or a village if close by when we were held up for road or bridge repairs. For a price one could find about anything one would need for this type of out of the way living places. We found the people and their stores were interesting and we could purchase staple groceries but fresh produce was at a premium. I had been quite amused about the answer a young clerk in a store in Whitehorse gave me when I asked her where the store got there bananas because they had an abundant supply. "Oh, we get them from the warehouse," she said, but beyond that she didn't know. We bought a full sack of bananas and other things that had been rationed during the war and not on the store shelves yet when we left San Diego.

Lodging for travelers was mostly crude camps that were leftovers from road construction gangs working on the highway. It was adequate shelter under the circumstances and spaced a long day's travel apart. We found it exciting to travel in pioneer territory knowing that perhaps in the not too distant future there will be tourist accommodations, motels, gas stations and trading posts along this highway.

Late one evening on arriving in Watson Lake we gassed up. Gassing up then meant pumping the gas from a barrel into a

Jerry can then pouring the gas into the car yourself. This was typical of all places on the highway where gas was sold.

Bud would always stop and help any one in trouble and sooner or later we'd meet them along the way. Some were traveling faster than we were. A fun couple we had helped get their overloaded car out of a ditch where it had slid on a rain muddy road, caught up with us and we had a party around the camp fire. They camped close to us by a lively gurgling stream and we pooled our food and after a big dinner they produced a jug of Canadian Club. The party lasted well into the night and no one was in a hurry to break camp and be on the way. Like us, they hadn't been to Alaska but had read some of the same stories we had and talked to service personnel who had served there during the war. Wonder what all those mama ducks and their little ones in the pond close by thought of all that off key singing?

One more night to camp and we crossed the border on the morrow. We made camp a short way off the highway close to a lively stream that would lull us to sleep as it gurgled over jumbled rocks. It was nearing midnight but still daylight and the last steady flow of uncomplimentary language directed to and about flat tires. A sharp rock, while crossing fresh gravel on the road, had put a three cornered tear in a good Jeep tire and was beyond repair. Finally the pounding and ringing of tire tools ceased and all was quiet when we crawled into our dusty sleeping bags—a fine dust that doesn't shake out. June 17. 1946 we reported to customs at the Canada-Alaska border. The chewing out we got from the Canadian officer for not reporting in to them on the date we had been given, didn't dim our enthusiasm. At Dawson Creek we had been given a permit for a certain number of days driving on the Alcan to the Alaska border. Canada didn't want the Mounties to have to spend time looking for people. We hadn't been in a hurry and had lingered in interesting places for a day or longer if we wanted to climb the hills, hike, or what ever the day dictated and forgot the time allocated on that permit. We knew where we were every day and the Canadian Mounties didn't have to come looking for us.

Thrill of thrills! We crossed the Canada-Alaska border and ate our lunch alongside the "Welcome To Alaska" sign. We were happy to be on U.S. soil again and the road is wider and smoother. The muskeg land and scraggly northern spruce didn't impress us but passing a few nice looking log cabins on cleared land did. The first "PRIVATE PROPERTY—NO TRESPASSING," sign we had seen since leaving the United States.

On reporting to the U.S. Customs at Tok they too wanted to know why we were so long overdue reporting there after leaving Dawson Creek. They were amused and let us go on to Fairbanks without a fine when Bud told them we were on our honeymoon and he was training his wife to the lifestyle she was faced with if his plans for a big game hunting business materialized in Alaska. "She might want to change her mind and fly back home from Fairbanks. We didn't know each other very well before I left for overseas duty and I didn't give her much time to change her mind about going to Alaska with me when I returned."

Our camp by the Tanana River, sure enough, those Alaska mosquitoes were big and fierce, gathering for a feast and our blood was the menu.

So soon after the war there wasn't a problem finding work in Fairbanks and wages were better than anything we had encountered in the work force back in the states. It was easier to get a job than it was to keep from going to work. There was a shortage of workers and businesses owners came to us. Bud went to work at Ladd Field on the outskirts of Fairbanks and I didn't have to ask for a job with a new business in Fairbanks—The Interior Decorating Shop. We moved into a very unmodern homestead cabin. The only place we could find to rent. Our pooled wages, that were not needed for daily living expenses, went for equipment we would need for bush living when we found what and where we would settle and start the business Bud planned.

During our first two years in Fairbanks there wasn't a back road or highway we hadn't explored. With our four wheel drive Jeep we could investigate about anyplace we wished to. If for a secluded fishing stream or a closer to work cabin to rent. Some one told us about a cabin we might rent if we could locate the owner who had left recently. It was only a trail down to a fairly decent log cabin but too narrow and swampy for the Jeep. I waited for Bud to investigate and he wasn't gone long before he came running back on that trail and a cloud of mosquitoes following him. He was outrunning them. Had he stumbled I am convinced they'd eaten him alive! I started up the Jeep and he jumped in and left them behind. He said it was a nice cabin but too close to a swamp where those mosquitoes bred and multiplied. We lost interest in that place immediately. I think I would have left on the next airplane for San Diego if he said we'd rent that cabin no matter even if it was a modern place with electricity and running water. Of course he had forgotten to put on bug dope.

It reminded me of a quote by Reuben Gains who had a popular radio program at the time. "Man has harnessed streams and rivers but the mosquitoes seems to have him baffled." Although some brilliant man made the bottle of mosquitoes repellant but who remembers to take it along? When you are parked by a gravel pit or a swampy stream and see some one come dashing out into the open from bushes pulling up their pants, running for their life, you know he forgot to take along the bottle of repellant.

Every weekend away from our jobs found us exploring mountains and trails within a radius of Fairbanks that we could leave right after work on Fridays and be back to work on Monday mornings. The one time we didn't make it back to work until Tuesday morning was when we explored the forty miles to the end of the Nabesna road which started at the Tok highway. Before WW II the Nabesna road was an extension from the Richardson highway at Glennallen. A truck road for hauling supplies to the Nabesna mine. (During the time the Alcan was being built the U.S. Army Engineers extended the road from the Nabesna Junction to Tok to connect with the Richardson highway and then on to Fairbanks. Which now has become the Tok Highway).

This country was too fascinating for us to turn back and the farther we drove the more we wanted to see. At one high point of the road (with the aid of binoculars) we looked across to a beautiful lake nestled at the base of high mountains of the Wrangell Range. Our map showed it to be Tanada Lake, with Copper Lake laying just beyond.

Bud and I both had a mutual interest in studying maps and we had checked all of Alaska's rivers and mountains. Always the Wrangell mountains held our interest. At the sight of these mountains and that big lake we knew we had to investigate there before any decision could be made. I had a feeling his mind was already made up to where he would start a big game hunting business. I liked Fairbanks and my work there and I wasn't too confident about a place as isolated as this would be but if we could get permission to live in that nice log cabin within two miles of the noted Nabesna mine then I would consider a winter there.

I should have known Bud well enough by this time to know he wouldn't give up until he located the owner of that cabin, for a small fee we had permission to live there come winter. It was too late for me to back out. I was about to get all the adventure I wanted and this was parallel to what I had already experienced on our way to Alaska.

It had been a weekend in early June when we made that first trip on the Nabesna road and knowing the road was not maintained in the winter months, we went ahead with plans and preparations. Having given our employers the required notice to quit our jobs, we were moved and were ready for winter by early October, 1950. Having lived close to a grocery store most of our lives, we of course, misjudged the amount of staple grocery items we'd need. We had made careful lists, gone over them carefully and assumed we had plenty of important supplies in the event of an unexpected emergency. "What if the snow is too deep for us to use the Jeep this winter if we want to drive out?" I asked. "No problem," Bud assured me, "we'll go by dog team."

Our first winter on the Nabesna Road in a comfortable log cabin with big picture windows looking out to towering mountain peaks was an ideal initiation to where our home on Tanada Lake was soon to be. One has to have a dog team in order to run a trap line and we had purchased five Huskies and a sled before leaving Fairbanks. It was a most interesting learning experience for us to harness up and run a sled dog team. They were experienced work dogs and we were amateurs and they knew it. Bud finally mastered the art of handling intelligent dogs bred to work but they were on vacation when I was the musher holding onto the handle bars of the sled. On nice days I enjoyed going with him when he checked his traps and with him yelling instructions to the dogs they let me be the driver for short periods on a good trail.

December arrived and so did a snow storm that lasted clear

into mid January and a cold arctic wind blew five and six foot drifts hard as concrete. The Jeep sat useless in those hard drifts as Bud and the dogs worked every day to make a trail, then it snowed heavier and the wind blew harder blotting out all evidence of their efforts. We were running short of the most important staples with a steady diet of moose meat, rabbit and ptarmigan. I missed my coffee and had no idea of how to make sourdough bread or pancakes with what remaining flour we had. We had plenty of corn-

On the way to Fairbanks

meal for the dogs and when we were out of flour I tried making things from corn meal but without baking powder it was tasteless. We were out of Blazo for the lamps and lifted a stove lid to play cards by the dim light and our radio batteries had gone dead. Those were long dark days in mid winter. The best laid plans can go astray as we all know. We had planned to spend Christmas with friends in Slana and would resupply at that time.

Our neighbor, an old timer who lived a mile beyond us and was caretaker for the mine and the only person living within thirty miles, had gone for his mail and groceries at Slana with his dog team before the storm hit and he couldn't get back. We were on our own.

We waited impatiently for the snow to settle (once it stopped snowing.) Then mid February the sun came out. We started out on the forty miles to Slana on a unbroken trail, the dogs pulled a heavy loaded sled with camping gear and what few groceries we had left. Corn meal and tallow for dog feed as well as the pot to cook it in.

Those five days with temperatures at 35 to 40 below zero every day was the toughest I hope I ever have to experience. As tough as Bud was he even played out at times when breaking trail on snowshoes for the dogs to follow. I had to follow on my snowshoes also but I had a chance to rest, sitting on the sled when he let the dogs rest while he was breaking trail. We'd set up a tent in the trees where there was plenty of wood for a camp fire. With warm sleeping bags we'd be warm and comfortable at nights. I'd get tired at times but Bud would encourage me to keep plodding along but if I'd trip and fall with my snowshoes on I couldn't get back on my feet without his help. I am sure it was just as well we hadn't heard of hypothermia, otherwise my story might have ended on this trip.

Chapter Three

Tanada Lake

My first trip over to Tanada Lake was early May, 1951 riding on the sled pulled by our dogs across seven miles of uneven clumps of frozen tundra. A real rough ride. We spent the long sunny days exploring the shore line of this frozen six mile long lake and made our overnight camp in a beautiful setting on a shore that was an ideal cabin sight that looked up to high mountain peaks where Dall sheep were peacefully grazing. I was "hooked" and we made our plans to build a log cabin on this lake.

Summer found us making the backpacking trip seven miles across the tundra flats from the Nabesna road to the lower end of Tanada Lake to Tanada Creek where the 14 foot AlumaCraft boat was waiting. Bud had hauled it over there on a sled while he could use the five dog team power on frozen tundra. It was necessary for us to outline the five acres we planned to apply for a business site before going to the BLM (Bureau Of Land Management), in Fairbanks. We spent a delicious few days on the hillside we chose doing this amateur surveying, marking what we estimated to be five acres. But most of those sunny warm days were spent planning and dreaming how we'd build a hunting lodge or exploring the surrounding canyons and steams. We were young and healthy, ambitious and we had a goal. Those seven miles across the tundra swamps was no obstacle for us. The towering, snow capped Wrangell Mountains were always within our sight.

The trip to Fairbanks to fill out the paper work at the BLM meant taking all five dogs with us as there was no one to leave them with while we were gone. This also meant taking camping gear and making camp where we could stay with and be close to the dogs. We couldn't stay with friends and our dogs too. I well remember some of those trips when four dogs could fit on top of gear in the Jeep when pretty white Wooly (our favorite) had to ride on top of the tarp covering gear in the small trailer. He'd cling for his life on rough roads or curves. I was always hoping Bud would choose a camp site and have the dogs tied before we drove into town. I'd feel embarrassed meeting all the people I knew. But not Bud. He was sure there would be better camping facilities on the opposite side of town.

We were so sure of getting our five acres here on Tanada Lake that when the three man survey crew flew out while they were still able to land with a floatplane, we had the trees cut and stumps dug out where the lodge was to be even their tent set up ready to cook for them. It was the agreement we'd furnish their room and board since it was such an isolated area. We were happy to oblige and it was an interesting two days for us especially with the latest news they brought as well as humorous stories. Little did we know at this time, that in 30 years this land would be in the Wrangell St Elias National Park and this five acres would be the only private land on Tanada Lake.

We would go by boat across the lake, spend the day cutting cabin logs. After a log was felled Bud used a tool called a peavey to get it out where he could winch it to the lake shore. My job with the peavey was to roll the log over if it got stuck.

It was two years of dedicated labor, cutting cabin logs, peeling the bark from them (my job) and towing them across the mile wide lake by boat to the cabin site. We had been living in an eight-by-eight foot white walled canvas tent before we could move into the luxury of our one room ten-by-ten-foot log cabin. Keeping a wood supply to feed a hungry stove, on cold winter days and nights, gave us all the extra exercise we needed. We had to use the tent canvas as a roof to the cabin until we could get slabs cut for a roof and floor. The floor was a variety of odds and ends of loose boards set across poles which Bud had flattened on one side as well as he could with the axe. One had to be careful walking on the floor as a loose board could flip up and whack you across the rear end. A misstep could put one foot down between the poles.

Hauling supplies all the way out from Anchorage with the

Jeep and trailer, then seven additional miles of tundra from the Nabesna road to the lower end of the lake and the last six miles to our cabin (using the dog team) kept supplies limited to the bare necessities.

The winter trail to Tanada lake was over a frozen trail and lake. In summer we took the boat with the dogs enjoying the ride to the lower end of the lake, then a seven-mile hike across the tundra to the Jeep parked on the Nabesna road. Every three weeks was about the average for a summer trip out for mail and groceries. Most of which was packed on our backs after leaving

Our log pile, getting ready to cut the roof and floor boards

the motorized transportation. We only had two dogs that would tolerate a pack to carry sugar, flour and cornmeal. If Bud wasn't leading one, me the other one, they would go for a swim and that wasn't good for flour or the sugar. Bud was the best pack dog on all those trips, carrying the heaviest and most of the supplies. This didn't allow for luxuries, no matter how small.

Those dogs knew the difference between when they were doing the work or riding with us in the Jeep or in the boat. Four dogs could crowd side by side behind us in the Jeep atop the tarp covered gear and if one crowded too much and got snapped at, it was up to me to turn around and settle them down. I got bit a couple of times by reaching between them at the wrong time, but nothing that didn't heal. Good natured fat Woolly rode atop the loaded trailer, otherwise all five rode in the empty trailer. This trailer had two wheels with open top and low sides. The all seemed to enjoy boat riding the most. On Tanada Creek, with Bud towing the fourteen-foot AlumaCraft boat, I'd swear they all had wide grins on their big mouths sitting up and looking very smug. The water in the creek was usually too low to operate the outboard motor so Bud put his hip boots on and with rope in hand, towed it the mile down stream to where the boat would be pulled up on the shore and covered with brush until our return. If we let the dogs run loose along the shore they would chase moose or whatever else they could stir up. One time when they were running loose our lead dog took after a cow moose and her little calf. We couldn't take a chance on that cow stomping that dumb dog to death. Bud, yelled his lungs out for Jim to "Get back here you stupid ———dog!!" He came right back out of the thick timber much faster than he went in with a very mad cow moose close at his heels. "Oh, oh!" who is going to get stomped?" I was excitedly watching from my safe spot in the boat close to shore and ready to push the boat out into the current if she wanted some of me also. The dog was smart and jumped into the boat, She went snorting right past Bud and turned to head back to the trees.

Another tremendous experience for a gal who was still learning the hard way about wilderness living was helping Bud whipsaw lumber. A generous friend gave us a whipsaw and explained to Bud how to build a whipsaw stand. First find four standing sturdy trees that are close together, cutting them off at six feet above their solid roots. They were to be three or four feet apart with a frame work at the top to allow a platform to stand on. Another holding crib atop of the other platform would hold the log to be marked thus allowing a space to pull the saw down through the log crib, (this description is meant for those who have never had the privilege or experience to use one). The end of the log to be ripped was marked with a chalk line for the width of board to be sawed. It sounded good to think we could cut our own boards for a floor and roof of the cabin. I was the flunky underneath who pulled the saw down through the log after the person on top pulled it back up. It would have worked a lot easier if Bud had chosen dry logs instead of half green which we discovered after a few real tough working days and still had nowhere near the amount of boards we needed. I'd get mad and tell him to do it himself when he would accuse me of dragging the saw when he was pulling it back up. He would come over to the log where I was pouting, then coax me

LeNora's on top just for the picture. Her job was underneath where all the saw dust came back down

back to work. I dearly wanted those boards for a roof and a floor so I'd go back to work until the next fight we'd get into over who was not doing what they were supposed to. I was still around when the last board was cut. I think it was two weeks after we started. I had resisted temptation NOT to be a bush pilot's wife if and when that dream of his materialized.

"If you ever plan to cut more lumber with a whipsaw, hire a strong man to help you," I told him, but I felt smug about what we had accomplished. Besides having a board roof with roofing paper to replace the canvas covering, now we wouldn't have to burn so much wood and could slow down the heat from escaping out through the ceiling.

For me it was much the same as it had been in earlier times when those women who went with their men and settled the west. Our cabin was lit by lantern, long dark winter nights, laundry done on a scrub board, baths in a round galvanized tub, clothes dried outdoors on a clothes line. I ironed my blouses and the pillow cases with "sad-irons" heated on the wood range as was water in a teakettle or a cooking pot. We had running water when I ran down the hill (bucket in hand) to a clear bubbling spring in summer time, or in winter, chopping a hole through five feet of ice, using a tool called an ice chisel (a metal pipe with a three-inch flattened end and sharpened like a chisel.) In summer our refrigerator was a five-gallon square tin (old aviation gas can) set in the cold spring water. My cupboards were wooden

The first cabin on Tanada Lake.

boxes that two five-gallon aviation-gas came in. The outhouse sat on a hillside looking out over the lake so it had no need for a door. Toilet paper didn't always take priority over food, so the old Sears catalogue ended up there. Wadding a single sheet in a closed fist softened it for a comfortable use (like I remembered from when I was a kid at home). Also a roll of toilet paper would roll to the bottom of the hill should you drop it.

I easily adjusted to living where there was a real variety of animals in there wild habitat. I especially loved it in spring when the moose and caribou cows were with their new born calves. The new little white Dall lambs frolicked on the mountain sides and on the lake a great many ducks and geese raising their young. Grayling and lake trout were plentiful and supplied a delicious meal for us when we took the time to catch them. Also there were grizzly bears, plenty of them at the time we moved into their country, we let them go there way and we were sure to stay out of there path. As long as they didn't bother us we had no intentions of disturbing their natural ways.

Ours was a subsistence way of life and wild meat and fish was an important part of our menu with sheep meat the deluxe dish no matter if steaks, roast or otherwise. Climbing the mountains to hunt the wild ram was a real vacation for us in comparison to the work we had been doing while looking

LeNora holding her black cat and trapped beaver hides and a fox.

forward to hunting season. Bud took on the task of teaching me to shoot his .30-06 rifle and I was good at hitting the target in the right place for a clean kill. Bud had collected two sheep previously and planned a hunt for me to shoot a Dall ram for meat supplement.

Always before leaving the cabin to go on a hunt, when we didn't want to take the dogs with us, we had to hide the gun the day before, out of their sight. They knew the difference and howled continually until our return unless we were going across the lake in the boat to work on the logs. The first time we went sheep hunting we could hear them from high on the mountain and I'm sure all the sheep within hearing were bound to be long gone from there.

Chapter Four

A Big Game Hunting Business in the Wrangell Mountains

To be in the big game hunting business on an isolated lake in virgin game country, an airplane was a necessity for transportation for us as well as our clients. We were into the beginning of a new era when small aircraft was replacing the outfitters who booked thirty day hunts, using pack and saddle horses in their business. Bud was eligible for financial assistance under the GI Bill. However, to get a pilot's license before we could buy an airplane, we had to spend a winter in Fairbanks with him taking flying lessons with a licensed instructor.

I was thinking if we can manage the finances I'll take flying lessons too. What an opportunity! I wonder what Bud will think about that? I can go back to work and if I have my own money I see no reason for his objection. If we are going to buy an airplane I'll use my money for flying lessons, otherwise it will help with the airplane payments and other expenses. Now will be my chance to fulfill a dream I have had as long as I can remember but it always seemed out of my reach.

I felt a twinge of sadness when leaving our log cabin home boarded up and bear proofed when we said goodbye but knowing we'd be back. We were on our way early in October before the ice started forming on the lake, now snow closed the Nabesna road for another winter. I was enthused about an airplane for transportation across that seven mile stretch of wicked tundra. Hopefully this would be our last trek across it with heavily loaded packs on our backs. My pack was always heavy with the books I included beyond the usual forty pounds and my disposition would be sour on reaching the cabin. But after two summers of walking, or should I say staggering, across those tussocks (sedge grass) growing in clumps two to eight inches apart. I got almost as good as Bud with his heavier pack. I had lots of experience in dancing on a polished floor, but dancing across those wobbly humps in order to keep my balance gave me a good excuse to use some of Bud's descriptive slang words when I fell down and he had to help me get back on my feet and lift my pack onto my back. The "Old-Timers" we were acquainted with had a name for this type of activity. They called it the "Tundra Hop." To me this tundra was only good for raising bugs & mice, of which there's already a super abundance.

My dream of taking flying lessons and flying our own airplane also was put on hold. I went to the same doctor that gave Bud his flight physical to get mine. I made the mistake of asking the doctor if I was starting to go through menopause. "Well let's have a look and find out why you're concerned", he answered. Then he took me totally by surprise with, "LeNora you are pregnant!!"

To say I was surprised was an understatement! That was the last thing I thought about or wanted to hear. What went through my mind right then was, "There went our dreams of a future in the hunting business. What will be Bud's reaction to this news? Will he go on without me? Will we both stay in Fairbanks or will he go back to Tanada Lake and I stay in Fairbanks?"

When Bud came to get me at the doctors office I could read the same questions that were going through his mind. Neither of us had much to say. We'd make plans as we went along.

The winter went fast with both of us working, me back to the Interior Decorating Shop and Bud back at Ladd Field. Bud was taking flying lessons whenever weather conditions permitted and his instructor was available. He finally got his pilot's license after much effort and a very patient instructor who frequently reminded him he wasn't running a bulldozer and to ease up on the controls. (The written test was the hardest for him.)

The extent of my flying was to go with him on cross country trips, after he had his license we'd rent a plane to go sightseeing or look at airplanes for sale. If the air was calm and all clear ahead he let me handle the controls for a short distance just to get the feel of handling an airplane.

At various times during the summer while living in Fairbanks we'd make a few days trip out to the cabin on Tanada

Lake and take what supplies we could to leave for a later time. Winter time Bud would freight supplies in with the dog team. We boarded with a new couple who had moved to a cabin on the Nabesna road. Under the circumstances I was delegated to spend my days in Fairbanks. I really didn't mind that. I enjoyed the work, the people and the activities.

I had been hearing the cliche about most babies in Alaska were born when the men were away from home, usually hunting or flying. Sure enough, my first fret and worry about Bud being overdue was when our baby was due. He had gone flying with a friend Johnny Cross. Two days later they still were not back. Before I went to the hospital I phoned a noted bushpilot, Randy Acord, asking him to fly out to where I thought they were camping. The pilot located them with no problem. They were standing by the airplane that was nosed into a ditch with a very bent prop. A borrowed mechanic and prop delivered to them that same day allowed Bud to arrive at the hospital ahead of his son.

At first sight of his red headed, bright-eyed son there was no question of what our future was to be. It would include our baby in our isolated home and future plans. Bud convinced me, with much persuasion, that babies do survive bush-living. I was skeptical. He was a healthy, lively baby and it would be a real challenge, but I had gone this far and might as well go on. There would be many adjustments we'd be faced with from now on.

We purchased a secondhand J-3 Piper Cub from a friend, Cleo McMahan, as well as a secondhand pickup. Bud had mastered an Alaska husky dog-team and now he needed flying experiences to master an airplane. Come spring and we were ready to return to Tanada Lake. Bud flew the airplane and I drove the pickup, me and our six month old baby.

We still had backpacking to do but only a fourth of a mile to Long Lake on the Nabesna Road. Bud could land on this lake with floats on the Piper Cub, or with skis on the winter ice. The majority of our supplies now were hauled with the pickup, then packed to the lake from the road where the pickup was left. A J-3 airplane is limited for space and weight, so I was left behind to keep packing what I felt he could carry on each trip as he ferried our purchases over to the cabin. When the last load was delivered it was my turn to fly home, a twenty-five-minute flight. I could never resist a smug feeling while looking below as we flew over that familiar tundra.

The opening day of the sheep hunting season in our area, I was in luck, a friend was at the lodge and would baby sit for us while Bud took me for a hike high on the mountain this beautiful fall day. The rams we had seen with binoculars were now even higher and I was proud of myself staying so close behind Bud until the shale slide we had to cross started sliding down hill with me on it. Bud had already crossed and was telling me to keep moving faster. It was closer to where I had started from than it was to him so I went back. I had made the mistake of looking a thousand feet down that slide to a huge pile of jumbled jagged rocks. Bud ran back across and took my hand and pulled me running across the width of the slide, which I estimated to be at least a hundred feet. He said it was just half of that.

Further on and around a rocky outcropping Bud peeked and motioned me to creep up closer and take a look. About 300 yards away stood one big ram. Bud was excited and motioning for me to get into position to shoot. Just to see that beautiful white ram in his own habitat I found myself reluctant to shoot. I just wanted to look at it, but it didn't wait for me to make up my mind. It turned and disappeared from sight but a smaller ram we hadn't seen jumped to his feet. I handed Bud the rifle and he was happy to oblige. He would have been unhappy with this novice hunter had we gone back off the mountain without any sheep meat. I was surprised he wasn't too disappointed not collecting those big horns.

What I really had on my mind I think, was carrying a heavy pack on my back going across that shale slide again and back down the steep hillside. Bud climbs like a mountain goat and runs across those shale slides they are an average of twenty feet across to solid ground. I am usually within calling distance behind him until one of those wide slides are in our path. They scare the hell out of me. I ask myself, "what I am doing up here?"

I didn't know at this time that I had missed my only chance for collecting a trophy Dall ram. A size that any sheep hunter would pay a big price to collect on a hunt and have it mounted and on display on the wall of his trophy room. Beside that, it was a memorable day, August 10th. My thirty-sixth-birthday.

"That's okay with me. I'll get one next year," I said, confident there would be next years. By that time Bud had the ram field dressed and packed on our packs, I was rested from the climb and had thoroughly enjoyed the beauty of the snow capped peaks and distant vistas. The air was clear and pure up here. Tanada Lake lay shimmering in the late afternoon sun with our cabin looking like a doll house nestled in the trees near the shore.

Bud was half way down the mountain and ahead of me, with the two back quarters and the head with horns still attached. It made for an unwieldy pack as he carried the rifle in his hand on the down hill side for balance. He was following a narrow sheep trail when he stepped on a loose rock. His pack shifted and over balanced him. He rolled a good ten feet and landed against a boulder. Unhurt but mad.

After I got over the shock of the unexpected but unhurt tumble, it gave me thoughts about what would I have done had he been seriously injured? How would I have gotten him to the cabin by myself or would I have to leave him there until I could hike out to the road and get help. Would he be dead when I got back? "Oh, you just worry too much. I'm not going to get hurt so bad I can't walk," was his most assuring comment when he was finished talking to the rock that tripped him.

Sheep roasts with bacon grease spread over it and roasted in the wood burning oven were delicious. The climb after one was well worth the effort. It was awhile before Bud trusted me to cook wild game steaks because he said I cremated them. It was a while before he caught on that I purposely didn't catch on very fast. I preferred his expertly cooked steaks. On the days we were across the lake working on the logs or sawmill he would put pinto beans, or a dinner of meat and vegetables, in his sheepherders Dutch oven buried in live coals in a hole in the ground and covered with live coals. It was a hearty meal.

I was glad I had a husband who was patient with my shortcomings and cooking never was one of my talents and especially no experience with wild game. One thing I refused to do was to help him skin or flesh the animals he trapped, or at a later date, the trophies the clients shot and yet it was our business to prepare them for the taxidermist.

What I did learn and was good at, was knitting socks. During trapping seasons I kept us both in hand knitted wool socks. Bud would bring the trapped animals in the warm kitchen (and bedroom combined) if they had to be thawed before skinning. A beaver, fox, mink or a wolf would be set atop a chair. Bud would spread a tarpaulin on the floor with the carcass and stretcher board. To insure I didn't have to look at it I would sit on the bed with my back turned from whatever animal shared the one room cabin. I would knit or read my precious, hard to come by books.

Acquiring our Cub spelled the end of their usefulness for our five huskies. We found good homes for them where they wouldn't be obliged to pull heavy sleds on cold winter trails. They were not young dogs when we got them. Their new owners wanted a sled dog team just for fun rides now and then to entertain friends and their kids. The dogs had been a useful part of our lives and I was fond of each one of them. They were my friends and I had confided in them like I would have with a human friend, had there been one around besides my busy husband. I forgave them for stopping at every bush to hoist a leg while their grins got wider looking back at me when, on occasions, I was the dog musher. Those rascals would not let me ride on the sled unless it was on a smooth trail or frozen lake. Otherwise when I'd be tired and get on the sled they would stop, pretending I was too heavy. If I got off and Bud hollered "mush" they were off at a fast pace. In remembrance I will miss them.

At a later time Bud made a successful bid on a surplus U.S. Army Weasel, (a tracked vehicle.) Because of his mechanical skills, we now had another mode of transportation to cross the tundra in winter and summer. With me steering the Jeep he towed it with the Weasel across the seven miles of tundra to the saw mill sight directly across the lake from our cabin. Now we could saw all the lumber we needed. The power takeoff unit on the Jeep was used for power to run the "one-man" saw mill a friend sold us. It ended up being a one woman as well as a one man saw mill. In summer when Bud wasn't flying fishermen to Tanada and Copper Lakes, we would be hauling logs in from the timbered bar and sawing lumber for a lodge and guest cabins.

We didn't always let work interfere with pleasure even though we both were dedicated to our projects. April twenty-second—

a memorable day—our eighth wedding anniversary. A calm, beautiful morning and Bud said if I'd hurry with the morning chores I could go flying with him. He didn't tell me his plans were for a flight in places where I had never flown with him before. I was pleased with this thoughtful surprise. I soon had extra diapers and emergency gear a baby needs, with baby on my lap, we were air-born and three happy people were at the beginning of a new day. This kid is a happy little fellow when flying and always looking out the window and knows all about what he sees way down below.

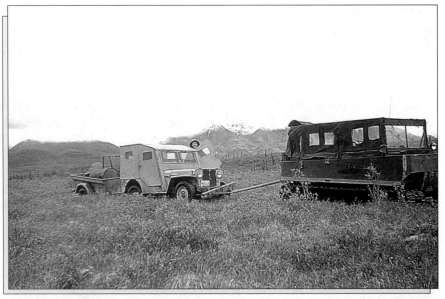

Our Army Weasel, towing the jeep we drove up the Alcan to our saw mill.

We flew over some of the most beautiful country I have ever seen in Alaska. We flew above Copper Glacier gaining altitude high enough to look for miles up the canyon where it birthed. Then flew completely around Black Mountain, while still in the Wrangells Bud pointed out six trophy Dall rams contentedly grazing in a high meadow. At a lower level a dozen or more caribou were grazing on a slope between the sparse and stunted northern spruce trees but plainly visible from the air. Clean and sleek looking animals. Two large bull moose, fat and contented looking, resting on an open windswept hillside undisturbed by their overhead observers.

What magnificent country we covered in an hours flying time without seeing a sign of another human being. It leaves me with a feeling of awe to be so privileged. Flying here and seeing this lavishly beautiful, unmatched and unspoiled wilderness, the animals that roam at will here leave me with a prayer that it will stay like this for generations to come.

Heading for Mount Sanford my pilot picked up the tracks in the snow of two wolves traveling together. We caught up with them and came in behind them flying low. Hearing the noise of the approaching plane those two big gray wolves put on a burst of speed and headed for timber, their luxurious gray fur rippling in the breeze.

Farther on we flew high over a lone moose sunning itself in the sunshine by a swampy lake. Circling a few times to watch a wolverine chasing a caribou cow in deep snow while the rest of the herd watched. We flew on when it gave up on that cow for a meal. Mount Sanford's eternally snow covered dome shone bright and clear in the distance as we headed home. This was an anniversary present I'll remember, from a husband who didn't have birthdays or anniversaries on his priority list.

By the time we had the accommodations and equipment ready and were catering to hunting and fishing clients, I was an experienced cook. I enjoyed and appreciated the compliments from the clients as well as pilots of visiting aircraft that dropped in from time to time; Fish and Game agents, other guide pilots and friends. The coffee pot was always on and there was always fresh cinnamon rolls or pie, most often blueberry. Those visiting airplanes took our mail out with them and they always had the latest news and most welcome conversation.

We had a battery operated radio we turned on only in the evening to get the news and messages that were aired after the evening news. Leaving the radio on for any length of time drained the battery and we had no way of charging it. KFAR radio station in Fairbanks and Northwind radio station in Anchorage had a message program that was aired for folks living in the "bush" without telephones. Anyone wishing to contact us other than by slow mail would send a message to "The Conkles at Tanada Lake" saying Bud should meet them, a party of two (however many would be waiting at Long Lake) and the time, that they wanted to go fishing, hunting or whatever the message was.

These programs were like an old friend coming to visit, especially for some one isolated like I was for days at a time or when Bud has been away longer than I expected and I'd be waiting word from him when he had a trip to Fairbanks or where he could get to a phone.

Now and then there was a message to someone that sounded so unusual you could hardly wait to find out what it was all about. One in particular sent this message; "To the guys at the airplane. I got out after a most unusual experience and some one will be there before dark. If it's dark start a bonfire so the helicopter can land."

A week later a Fish & Wildlife airplane landed and told about an airplane flying up from the Lower 48. It was heading for Anchorage and had crashed about an hour after checking in at Northway Flight Station. There were four men in the plane but no one was hurt in the emergency landing. The tundra looked like a smooth field to the pilot when engine trouble developed. One man volunteered to walk out for help. On their map the Slana River didn't look very far away and was close to the Tok Highway. He was following a moose trail when a grizzly came running up behind him and right over him, knocking him down but kept on going like it was after something else. That shook him up real good. When he got to the Slana River it was running full and he took off his clothes to swim across. As he was holding his clothes high out of the water, a tree branch, moving fast in the swift water, caught his clothes and he was unable to swim fast enough to retrieve them. Standing naked alongside the Tok Highway trying to flag down a passing car, but no one stopped. They thought it was that 'crazy guy' who lived back in the woods. When a car did finally stop to pick him up he got to a phone to let his friends know he made it and to send help.

Every one involved always listened faithfully to these messages in the event they had a message. Many of these messages were entertaining regardless if not for them. Some were pure comical;

"To my sister Paula, my brother Gene he died I think, but I got a letter from him yesterday and he not died. He think maybe he died because he was in a car wreck and now in the hospital."

"To my husband Joe out moose hunting. I am in the hospital. I am sick a little bit."

"To my daughter Patty, I had a dream. I think you died. Call me and tell me if you did not die."

"To my husband John out on the mountain sheep hunting, I hope you have your sheep and come home soon because I wrecked the car today but it still runs."

If you were interested in the outcome of these messages you waited for the next installment. It was easy to detect a school girls message to a boy friend out in the bush, or a wife to hubby; especially during hunting season. The messages always had greetings from the kids and problems that mama couldn't solve while he was away. Always there was one or more telling their man the baby had arrived.

One day I was baking bread in the kitchen and went out to see what Bud was hollering about on the porch. He was really snorting because I had chopped a bone in half with the sharpest side on his double-bladed axe. I got a lecture about I should use the meat saw instead of the axe on frozen meat. I told him if he would saw off the steaks, or a roast, from the frozen leg of a moose before he went aerial wolf hunting then I wouldn't need the axe to chop bone. Besides, now I am even with you for cutting your tough old toe nails with my sharp sewing scissors. You know I do not so much as cut paper with them." A pregnant silence ended the day that happening occurred.

Everything grinds to slow motion when deep winter sets in. Now we have a small shed with a wood burning heater stove where Bud can do machinery, boat and motor repairs and a limited amount of aircraft repairs. We are burning wood for three stoves now that we have the addition finished for the living room, that means spending a lot of hours getting the winters wood supply. From Bud's practical thinking, it saves on wood to put a tarp down on the living room floor to do small repairs or to skin the animals he catches in his traps. He enjoys aerial wolf hunting moreso now that he has the airplane than he did when trapping. He returns with a wolf to skin now and then but I tell him I think he consumes more aviation-gas and time, besides the hours charged to engine time on the Cub. He prefers to think the price he gets for the hides more than covers that cost. I'm not convinced.

Those big Alaska timber wolves average a hundred pounds or more and most of the hides stretch about seven feet, and each one in prime condition. They look real neat on stretchers to dry and set back in a corner away from the heat. There was a time I would have been emphatic about him skinning an animal or repairing tires and engines in our small kitchen but the bitter cold winter days I only complain when it is a stinking wolf that has been eating something terribly decayed. If he can stand it while working that close, then I can too for a short while. I can enjoy his company while he works. He tells me of his day, where he flew, what he saw and about the wolf he spotted, tumbled and landing to retrieve it.

One winter day a friend landed his Super Cub at our cabin. He had been looking for a pack of wolves that were reported to be in an area some distance from Tanada Lake but didn't find them, so stopped in to visit us. The two men were talking trapping, flying experiences, and all those things men like to talk about. When I had the chance I asked him if he had a garage or shed where he did his skinning jobs. "Oh definitely. No way would I be allowed in any room of the house doing a job like that," was his answer. "LeNora frowns visibly but accepts me doing the job in the house sometimes," Bud told him, and I was pleased to hear I was such a congenial wife.

We went on to tell him about some friends of ours who were gold miners but he also trapped in the winter months. His wife told us about the first wolf he caught when they had arrived in Alaska. They only had a one-room cabin at the time. He hung the wolf from a rafter and while skinning it he kept turning it around. Instead of him moving around the carcass. He let go to get up to stretch and of course it started unwinding and squirting blood in a circle all around the log wall interior over everything; bed, stove, dishes and clothes. What a mess they had to clean up. He was obligated to put a stove in a tent and do any further skinning jobs there or spend the winter without his cook and mining partner.

A young couple had moved to a small lake close to the Nabesna road, about twenty miles from the Tok Highway and applied for land to build their cabin. This lake was good for landing with skis and a light load. They were always happy to have us stop in to visit, but especially when they could keep our little son for us if I wanted to go flying with Bud. Most times our little one went with us on my lap. He was too active a child to anchor him onto the gear piled up behind my seat.

Bud could sense it when I was grumpy and had been in-doors too long and he'd take me flying with him to go for the mail or just flying around someplace. I loved to go flying with him and was ready to go at any time. I was confident I'd make a good gunner for him if he'd take me aerial wolf hunting. I tried to convince him I could shoot from the airplane without getting excited and shooting through a lift strut or the propeller. He finally consented to let me try but only after a long briefing

A big game guide in the making.

of what not to do, how to do it, especially not to hold a loaded shot gun aimed at the back of the pilot's head. I had listened to many pilots, when they were together telling of the experiences they had had with gunners or even themselves, discussing everything that did or could happen. There was the story Bud would tell about shooting himself down when he hadn't had the J-3 very long and not very much experience as his own gunner. (That story was told in an early issue of the *ALASKA SPORTSMAN* and the book *TRAIL OF THE EAGLE*).

Was it just my luck we never caught up with wolves when I

was flying with him and was to be the gunner? Or did he purposely know where to avoid finding any? Or maybe he didn't
have the confidence I had in my shooting? I wanted the opportunity to know I could, even if my pilot wasn't sure enough to
take a chance. Bud was husband-wise enough to avoid a con-
frontation on that subject knowing I'd remind him of some of
the gunners he took hunting who didn't hit a running wolf no
matter how many passes he flew over it. Also, I wasn't beyond
reminding him of the time he accidentally shot off the tip of the
propeller instead of the wolf.

Chapter Five

A New Super Cub

Business was good and Bud had been doing a lot of flying so it was time for the semiannual inspection on the J-3 Cub. That was always done in Fairbanks. At Bachner's Aircraft Service two new Super Cubs had arrived a few days before. Jess Bachner offered Bud a real deal on a trade-in and Bud was confident our "friendly banker" would finance the balance but he had

The new Super Cub, tied to shore in front of Tanada Lake Lodge

to come back to Tanada Lake to get me. The bank wasn't too eager to finance the new airplane, definitely not without my signature. Since I was the one who did the book work, I hurriedly gathered

Oh, oh. Pilot error. The new Super Cub through the ice on Tanada Lake.

up all papers to show our finances and why we thought we could make the heavy payments the bank would require. Bud wanted that new Super Cub and between the two of us we persuaded the bank and Bachners that we could make the payments.

We were detained in Fairbanks most of the week for Bud to get checked out for flying the different aircraft. It was a good few days for me, while staying with some of our good friends, to visit around, show off the baby like all proud parents always do. The day we were to fly home it was windy in Isabel Pass in the Alaska Range. I was glad it wasn't the J-3 because those heavy wind gusts tossed that Super Cub up and down and even side ways. That flight convinced me Bud was capable of handling as tough a situation as we were in until out of the Pass and into calm air. I was thinking, at the time, when watching the expression on Bud's face while handling the controls, this guy can handle it so best I not spend time worrying when ever he is flying.

"Now," I told myself, "I'm sure you will not resent our new Super Cub taking priority over everything I think I need, now I won't have to stay home all the time to take care of the baby." This airplane with a 150 HP Lycoming engine can out perform the smaller J-3 with only an 85 HP engine, we can now take the baby and all the required accouterments with us when we make the flights out to the highway for supplies and mail, which is an average of twice a month.

With the fishing business in summer and the hunting business in the fall, business was very brisk. Besides an active baby to care for, I was constantly cooking for fishermen and hunters, cabins to take care of, packing the groceries for the clients and their guides during hunting season, then there was the book work and correspondence. We were starting to book hunters two years in advance of their hunt so most of the correspondence was taken care of in the winter months. Bud was flying long hours each day unless he was on a guided hunt with a client. We booked clients for spring and fall hunts on the Alaska Peninsula and he'd be gone for weeks at a time while I'd be at the lodge to keep things going until his return.

The only improvements at Tanada Lake Lodge was the new Majestic wood range. A real improvement over a small Yukon camp stove and a Coleman three burner propane stove. I was very happy with my new stove and enjoyed baking pies and breads. Many a time I was cooking for as many as ten or twelve men at a time at the table, breakfast and dinner.

One day we were returning on a flight from Slana for mail and groceries and had been gone overnight due to flying weather. As we flew close to the cabin a grizzly bear exited the door and bounded across the tundra flat heading for timber. It must have recognized the buzzing of the airplane and put on more speed as Bud flew over it trying to see what it was carrying away. The Cub was on floats and it took time to land in the lake and taxi to shore before getting to the cabin to see what that uninvited bear had for dinner. The mess inside wasn't as bad as anticipated but the flour, sugar, salt and canned peaches all mixed together was a total loss. The one pound can of Darigold butter had to be what that rascal carried away because Bud never did find the can. We decided the bear hadn't been in the kitchen long enough to lick all the butter out of the can so carried it away with him. Another indication it hadn't been inside long because it went back out the door instead of a window. Normally a cabin "break in grizzly" will go in one window and out another. We had seen this one on the shore across the lake and on a hillside and in berry patches so often we had named it "Disappearing Willie," because it was nowhere in country when bear season was open. A spring and fall hunting season passed and he was still around.

"I'll get that rascal if he ever comes in my kitchen again, unless of course you get him first," I told Bud while we were cleaning up the sticky gooey mess. "Everything we have here is too hard earned and that bear can find some place else to eat."

That was the first time, but not the last break in. When a bear has been in a cabin there is an awful mess to clean up. They often tear a cabin apart.

This bear ripped the 2 x 4 timber brace off the barred door that Bud thought was bear proof. Once a bear gets into a cabin and finds food, they will return and they are so strong it's hard to keep them out. So best they are eliminated. Bud had hunters booked who would be very pleased to collect that grizzly's trophy black hide come September but I kept the .30-06 rifle loaded for bear and real handy.

"Disappearing Willie" came back one dark night and was planning a feast of fresh moose meat Bud had hung in the shed to age and had left the door open. He tied the dog with its chain to the tree close to the kitchen door. During the night I heard the dog let out a loud, scared "woof," then silence. Bud jumped out of bed and opened the door and flashed the light around and no dog; just a snapped chain. Then two eyes in the bushes a few yards from the shed.

"You cover me while I close the door on the shed, "my brave husband said handing me the 300 Magnum rifle." That grizz' isn't going to get that meat I packed out of the woods, then into and back out of the airplane and uphill to the shed."

"When I was hanging out clothes this morning I saw a bear way high on the hillside. I looked with the binoculars and I'm sure it was "Disappearing Willie" but you never believe me when I say I saw a big bear. That bear is closer to the meat than you are, so are you sure I'll hit the bear if you both get to the shed at the same time?" I was trying to convince him to wait for daylight.

We didn't want a wounded bear around so shooting over the direction he had last seen glowing eyes was out. Yelling at it, banging pans kept us busy half the night, when no more eyes shone in the flashlights beam Bud then left me at the cabin door, rifle in hand, while he went to close the door of the shed and put cans in front to make a noise if the bear came back and tried to get in. I wasn't as confident as he was and preferred to let the bear have the moose meat. He could get more meat but could I get another husband? That had been a long night. For days after that my head went around in circles every time I went out doors thinking that bear would come back, but it didn't. The dog had no intentions of protecting his providers. When Bud found him the next day he was hiding in a far corner under a bed in one of the of the cabins. "Disappearing Willie" made the mistake of not checking the calender. It was the last day of the spring bear hunting season, one lucky hunter just happened along.

I didn't mind living in bear country as long as the bears were far away, far enough away that I had to use binoculars to see them. I preferred to be away from home if a grizzly bear wanted in or around our cabin, unless my brave husband was beside me. Especially now with a small child around.

Being a hunting guide, Bud always stayed calm and knew

what to do to keep his hide intact from the many close calls he had with grizzlies but I still had much to learn. Grizzlies were plentiful around the lake in the spring when the ice went out and salmon spawned, died and washed ashore. We could avoid the bears because they were in the open and we'd see them before they saw us. It took me a long time to realize there wasn't a bear lurking in hidden places waiting to jump out at me. I enjoyed being out in the berry patches too much to stay indoors but always kept my rifle close by.

I also had to train myself to stop worrying about bears eating my little son. He was hardly more than a year old and instead of walking he ran. The sandy beach just out of my sight from the kitchen window was the place he preferred to play with his trucks and toy airplanes. "More sand and beach here," was his argument.

I'd get plenty of exercise running down the hill checking on him. I had a busy schedule with the chores of a "bush wife" routines, besides checking on a happy little boy playing and amusing himself, trying to convince his mother he wasn't afraid of bears. Two different times I had found fresh bear tracks where he had been playing. Were they someplace watching him at play and not a threat to them, just curious? I had heard of times when a curious bear watched a child playing while unaware of the bear until a parent or grown up called the child in. I wanted to convince myself that like his daddy, no bear was going to carry him off. It was always when Bud was gone for the day or longer that I'd spend more time trying to find him when he'd wondered away from his allowed limits. He didn't like to be fenced in. I guess he came by freedom naturally!

With an active child around there is bound to be an emergency sooner or later. The first one happened when Colin was still a toddler and his daddy had built him a toy airplane with a propeller and even a play instrument panel. It was Colin's favorite toy and he spent hours in the cockpit after spinning the prop and pretending he was really flying. I was in the kitchen baking cinnamon rolls with raisins and had given him a few in his hand. He had gone back to his airplane and soon came running back in the kitchen choking. I looked down his throat and thought I saw a raisin, turned him upside down, swatted his back and nothing came out. He seemed okay the rest of the evening.

Bud was flying and not due back until the following day. I wasn't too concerned until the little guy started vomiting green bile during the night. I guess it was mental telepathy because Bud flew back at daylight. We loaded a few things in the new Cub and flew down to Slana. The Cub was on skis and no brakes, so landing on the ice covered road, it was urgent that he stop the airplane. When it looked like it wasn't going to stop in time, Bud jumped out of the airplane and dug his boot heels in the ice to slow the plane down, but it slid on the road a few feet and we still ended up in the ditch. Lucky no damage that kept the plane from flying and friends helped get it back on the road and parked.

At this time the Tenth Rescue Squadron airplane from Ladd Field (in Fairbanks) would be dispatched to all outlying districts for all emergencies. When I phoned the doctor with an emergency, Dr. Weston told me to take our son to Tok and he would send the rescue plane on to Tok. At the time there was only a bush pilot's landing field there, with no lighting. The town people would be alerted to shine the headlights of their cars down the runway for a plane to land.

Hours had passed and the child didn't seem to be worsening. When he asked to go potty I sat him on a coffee can. The sound of a metal ping hitting the can solved the problem. That kid had swallowed a sharp metal piece from the instrument panel of his toy plane. It was only a fourth of an inch long and had a long sharp point (to hold it in the wooden interment panel). We flew back home after canceling the rescue plane and the flight to Tok. As time went on that wasn't the only emergency that all three of us survived. We would cope, but my hair just got more gray.

Airplanes are a responsibility and demand attention when the wind picks up. Tiedown ropes are checked to be sure they will hold, besides all the rest of the major attention if a pilot plans to fly an undamaged airplane. Bud had taken the weasel out to the road to haul freight back from the pickup parked on the Nabesna Road and he would be gone overnight. The airplane was my responsibility until his return. I was reminded, emphatically, should the wind pick up while he was gone I was to be sure to check the plane and the tiedown ropes. The plane was sitting on ice and some times the ropes will loosen. He hadn't been much more than out of sight (and yelling distance) when I heard water gurgling and rushing (as in a fast stream.) I dashed to the lake shore in time to see water spouting five feet in the air less than five feet beyond the airplane. This is called a water spout and is caused by pressure building up under thick ice. It was a long two hours I stood helplessly watching the water creep insidiously around the skis and close to shore. I stood debating what action I should take, move the Cub before the skis were flooded then frozen in ice, or should I attempt to untie and turn it into the wind that had risen to strong gusts? I was doubtful I could handle it by myself and it even crossed my mind to start it up and taxi it farther away from shore. That could likely be a disaster. Or should I just stand by and wait for the worst to happen? It was early April and the nights were still freezing, there was no use in me standing there all night freezing too so I decided a "frozen in" airplane was better than one bouncing around the lake so I went to bed! I might as well have saved myself all that worry because that prodigious problem solved itself. At daylight I was apprehensive what I'd see. The wind had died down, the gushing water had stopped and all the overflow moved back into the lake through the ice cracks.

There was another winter day when Bud was away and not expected back until the following day. During the night a warm wind started up and the wire loops (which were frozen into the ice and held the tiedown ropes attached to the wings) melted loose and left the new Super Cub untethered. The wind was rising and I jumped out of bed to go check on the plane in the early morning. "Oh, Oh, I'm in trouble now!" I was thinking. I wasn't sure I could handle this job I was faced with but I managed to roll two fifty five gallon drums of aviation gas down the few feet from the shed and had both wings anchored before wind gusts became so strong that any one of them could have flipped the plane onto its back. The long wings can easily catch the power from each strong gust of wind.

I had a feeling I might have been mad enough to start walking with my bundle of clothes on my back had I let my competition get wrecked and he scolded me for not taking care of it. I was mostly mad because Bud had forgotten to leave those drums closer to the airplane in the event I needed them.

All the wives I personally knew whose husbands flew Super

Cubs, likely other type aircraft too, knew we were second to his beloved airplane. Airplane parts are expensive and frequently needed so they take priority over the wife's wants. Getting started in a business with limited funds meant the wife did without.

I was beginning to think I worried more over the airplane when it was my responsibility than I did over my husband when he was long overdue getting home. It was a real responsibility too when I was his flight plan and knew where he went and when he was due to return. I'd allow for a variety of delays before I'd let myself start thinking he'd had an accident and how long would it be before I would know? Unless he was someplace where he could send me a message via radio I had no way of knowing.

Bud's standard answer when he'd return and I had spent a long time fretting and wondering was "Well I knew where I was all the time and the weather was so bad even the ducks and carrier pigeons were walking. I tried to catch a moose to take a message to you."

"Gee thanks for that information. How long am I supposed to wait here before I start walking out to the Nabesna road to the pickup?"

The monthly payments to the bank kept us figuring how to survive on what money was left from the summer fishing and fall hunting, but now the polar bear hunts out of Barrow added greatly to our income. The summer of 1964 Bud made enough money from his share of the proceeds, flying the Super Cub spotting fish for the boat, The Valiant Maid, out of Cordova. Now we were able to pay off the loan from the bank. Buying pontoons, skis and the big tundra tires added much to the total. We lived very frugally those years when the payments we were obligated for didn't include insurance for the airplane. We were thankful we still had no damage at the end of that fishing season. Bad weather is always to be reckoned with. Three times in a storm it was very close to being overturned (out on rough water). One calm night when all the crew was sleeping soundly after many hours of hauling in fish, the winds came up and the ropes that anchored the airplane alongside the boat came loose, Bud awoke and dashed up on deck, there was no airplane. Too dark to locate it and the spotlight on the boat didn't pick it up along the shore where he expected to see it pounded to junk. No one had an explanation as to how it had drifted around a rocky point and was sitting on quiet water in a sheltered cove. How lucky can one be? I was at the lodge and had fishing customers to cook for so didn't have time to worry about Bud or the airplane.

We had customers who flew their own airplanes to Tanada Lake, rented one of our cabins and I cooked their meals. A pilot friend, C. B. McMahan, flew some of our clients in from a lake near the highway and would come back to fly them back out again when he had time from his busy summer schedule. He did this while Bud was spotting fish for a boat in Cordova. When all our summer obligations were taken care of and the last fishing client flown out, I was ready for

Some guests flew their own aircraft to the lodge.

the pilot to come back and fly me and Colin out to Long Lake where the pickup was parked. I purposely hadn't booked any more customers until hunting season, by then we both had to return.

We drove to Gulkana, with a few stops along the way to visit friends and after an overnight stop we boarded Cordova Airlines and flew to Cordova. We stayed and enjoyed the town and its activities and the people until Bud was finished on his job then we flew back with him. A great scenery trip I'd likely never see otherwise. There was plenty of work could have been done had I chosen to stay at home but I was ready to see some place different.

Airplanes use aviation gas and oil. Other equipment will use regular gas and oil (aside from repairs) and all this has to be hauled up from Valdez, always a two day trip that has to be scheduled at convenient times when we be could be away from home. Winter trips over Thompson Pass could be a challenge as well as unexpected happenings. Weather would be unpredictable and roads closed due to high winds and drifting snow. We hauled gas in 55 gallon drums, two in the trailer and four in the pickup.

One memorable trip over Thompson Pass in deep winter we had checked the weather and it was favorable. The closer we got to where we'd start climbing we noticed the absence of trucks on the road. The higher we went the higher were the drifts alongside the road and the road was too narrow to turn around if a truck was coming down off the summit. Talk about sweating out the half hour or so to the summit and meeting a truck in a convenient place to pass (knowing who would have to back up on the narrow road)! A truck driver told Bud the road was good on down the steep grade to Valdez but all traffic on the side we had just come up was stopped until the Highway Department notified the roadhouse at the foot of the mountain that it was clear to go on over. Bud was plenty upset that there was no signs anywhere on the highway to alert traffic. We were the last ones and there was no more truck traffic behind us. That could very well have been an accident looking for a place to happen.

On the return trip we were driving in a swirling snow storm and following the lights of a fuel truck ahead of us. The strobe light on the truck was all that was visible in the blowing snow. A half mile or more from the summit a tire chain came off our rear tire. Bud heard it hit the trailer and not wanting to lose it he told me to jump out and pick it up. The road was so icy he'd spin out, with that load on he'd never get started again. He yelled, "wait for me at the summit." The pickup was moving so slow I jumped out without losing my balance, went back away in that wind and blowing snow and found the chain. A truck coming up caught up with me and was thoroughly startled when

I appeared out of the swirling snow like an apparition. I waved him on and yelled I was okay. I knew he would spin-out if he stopped. Bud was there at the top, now he knew why I was walking. He told Bud it sure startled him to see someone appear out of snow like that, he thought he had partied too much the night before.

"Another job for a dutiful wife," I told him. "Tire chains cost money and Bud didn't want to lose it."

I didn't see how Bud had loaded the trailer after he bought the roofing paper in Valdez, but when we returned and were unloading, one roll was missing! How could it have fallen off the trailer? I guess on the rough roads we traveled on. We needed that roll to finish the roof on the bedroom. When the weather warms up to zero or it snows, the room is warm from heat inside, it starts to drip like rain from the condensation in the ceiling. Bud had put a plastic tarp over the places where the wind had torn the tar paper off, but it cracks and leaks. Trying to control this situation we had taken the one pound tin cans butter came in, cut the round top and bottoms out and used the flattened sides to nail down the tar paper edges of the roof. We'd get winds so strong they could find a weak spot and start tearing paper loose. We have a canopy over our beds (and a can-o-pee under our bed), of light blue plastic so it doesn't drip on our bed. We have enough drips living in this house.

Using the Weasel and sled getting our winter's wood supply was easier to accomplish now. With the barrel stove in the cabin it was much appreciated and enjoyed. The 18X20 foot log addition could be kept warm. I now had the kitchen range free of the many winter items that had to be kept there. Now lapping around the iron legs of the barrel stove is the drained oil for the airplane engine, the battery, his heavy mukluks, shoepacks, flying pants, as well as anything else he may need that can't be left outside to freeze. I was used to all this now. Like everything else in life you accept and live with it and every improvement is a pleasure and not taken for granted.

I remember the winter before how happy I was when he finished an engine he was rebuilding, I think it was for the Weasel, he lovingly wrapped it in a tarp and took it out to the shed.

After he gathered up all of his tools and cans of bolts, I cleaned the floor and hung the new colorful curtains. I had material I bought one time on one of my few shopping trips someplace and had them finished and ready. Now, instead of a garage, I told Bud; "It looks more like a woman lives here." He agreed.

While at Tanada Lake the deep winter's cold wasn't as bad as the winds that blew straight down between the two mountain peaks to the south of us and across the lake. It would be 40 below zero on the thermometer on the window outside, but nice and warm inside. This was another time Bud was staying indoors but he's restless when he can't fly and checking the traps he has set, go aerial wolf hunting, or even for the mail and groceries. Five days of blizzard winds and when the wind diminished to only an occasional gusts, he was out of bed at daylight and for an hour would dig the skis out from hard snow drifts that had them imprisoned up to the Super Cub's belly. The snow and wind gusts blew out the plumbers torch he used to heat the engine. My job was to stand in the wind, hold the engine cover (a canvas tarp that reaches to the ground), to keep the wind from blowing the tarp into the flame and catching the engine on fire. Bud has decided he'd wait no longer to go for the mail.

Twice I hear him taxi out and return, the motor sputtering and trying to quit. He returned, tied the plane down and returned to the cabin to inform me he has to work on the carburetor. He thinks snow may be the problem. I couldn't tell from looking out a window what he was doing with the engine cowling up but I could hear him using cuss words he often uses and some I had never heard before. Definitely not at the airplane but the gusts that blew snow into the engine after he had cleaned it out. An hour later he was taxiing out to warm up the engine, then in the air to circle and fly over the cabin to let me know he was on his way. The last I saw of the Cub it was winging its way across the lake, over and around the mountain and out of my sight. The motor sounding clear and steady.

I pray for his safe return as I always do when he flies away. I feel a bit apprehensive and hope it was only snow that ailed the motor another morning and I'll patiently wait for his return with any interesting mail. I look at my sleeping baby and realize we are alone with only the wild animals and uncounted miles. If he doesn't return…?

A long busy day for me, looking out the window frequently and hoping to hear the welcome sound of the returning plane. Then total darkness and I knew he would not be back until morning. The wind had died and I thought he would pick up the mail and a few groceries and be back long before dark, although the days are short this time of the year. I can't help but wonder why he isn't back. I try not to be concerned.

The lake is booming and thundering; encased in its five foot thick ice prison. A cold clear night with brilliant stars sparkling in a dark sky. From the tree on the hillside behind the cabin comes the resonant voice of the owl that lives there, a bird of wisdom…so what is he telling me? "Hoo-hoo-oo-oo," then a hush. Soon the owl's call came again. Then there was silence. Inside the house was quiet as a mouse wetting on a bit of cotton. I miss the singing howls of the Huskies. I'd like to have them all in here with me. Baby sleeping soundly after his busy day, the fires are stoked, I read a while, an adventure story, my mind drifts away and I wonder if he is safe on the ground. I know he carries emergency gear and why should I worry? He'll be back and then I'll know why he didn't come back before dark but still I wonder. My book doesn't hold my interest so I go to bed and sleep. I can't do otherwise.

Late afternoon of the next day he over flew the cabin to let me know he was back. I put mine and Colin's parkas on and we were down to meet him by the time he had taxied to the tie-downs. I helped him drag a big old dog wolf back up the steep bank to the cabin. This one was frozen and difficult to drag. He had another one he had rough skinned where it fell and would finish it in the cabin. I was so happy to have him back home safe after all the things I had imagined could happen that I gladly shared the living room for the work he had ahead of him. (I didn't complain that this one did stink.) It had been eating on a moose that had been dead for awhile. Quite awhile I'm willing to bet.

The story that took him so long to come back home went something like this: After he picked up the mail and groceries at Slana he wanted to have a look in an area quite a distance away where some one at the post office told him a pack of wolves had killed a moose. He didn't find the pack but after flying around a bit he caught two wolves out on an open flat. He dropped one and finally caught up with the other one, it was close to the timber when he shot at it. He had landed back at the first one he shot, roughly skinned it, then spent time looking for the other one where it had gone into the trees. It was getting dark so he made himself a comfortable over night camp. He spent all the next day looking for the wolf because he knew he had hit it, as revealed by blood on the trail. When he did finally find it the wolf had died and was frozen stiff. It was a time consuming project to drag it through the thick brush and back to the airplane. It was also a project getting them into the plane so he could fly home.

As if it wasn't enough for me to worry about a husband when he was too long overdue, one of the longest hours I can remember was the afternoon my thirteen month old baby flew with his daddy in the airplane. Bud was loading the plane and had a passenger to fly out to the Nabesna Road. Colin crawled up in the baggage compartment behind the passenger seat. Bud tried to lift him out but he hung onto a brace and was determined to fly out to Long Lake with his friend Mildred. She and her husband had been fishing on Tanada Lake and staying with us. They were some of our favorite customers and she and Colin were good friends. Colin insisted on waiting at the road with her while Bud returned to fly him out. I couldn't believe all the things I imagined happening to both of them and the airplane in that hour they were gone and until the Cub returned with a happy little red head sitting proudly in the passenger seat with his seat belt fastened. It was the first time he had flown in the airplane without me. Over the years I'd get used to him flying with his daddy and always their safe return.

When Colin was fifteen months old we took him with us on a scouting expedition in the sheep hills. Bud had a client booked for a sheep hunt on the opening day that coming August. He wanted to look in a new area where he had previously seen some real trophy rams. I wanted to go too because he would be landing on a lake where I planned to camp and wait for him. Sounded good in the planning but knowing Bud he always wanted to go farther or stay longer. I always wanted to go along afraid I'd miss something. From past experiences we always took along extra groceries.

Our tent was set up on the bank of a lovely lake at the foot of steep hills, Bud left early the next morning and Colin and I amused ourselves picking blueberries on the hillsides but mostly I was climbing farther up a hill to catch him and head him back down before he went clear to the top. Late that afternoon Bud was back and said first thing in the morning we'd all go but we'll take a different route back down a canyon to this lake and the airplane. I never question his judgment and willingly went along.

Bud carried Colin in the canvas bag of his Trapper Nelson packboard where this kid has had more rides than most babies do in a baby buggy. He rode like the little trooper he is. We had crossed over the top of the first peak, gone up a canyon and started climbing a second. Then it started raining and fog was coming in. Bud said if we went around a point we'd come out in a low valley and it was a shorter route back to the airplane.

We were in some rugged wet country—the rain was making rocks and grass slippery. Bud was ahead of me and maneuvered around a sharp rock outcropping across a wide shale slide and with all the jumping up and down in the pack on his back he could easily become over balanced. I had visions of both of them tumbling down into the canyon below. I stood watching and agonizing until they were safely across. They made it and so did I but I promised myself it would be the last time for taking a baby on a mountain climb. We'd just wait until he was old enough to use his own two feet. I wondered afterwards how long it would have taken some one to miss us if we hadn't returned on the date we had said we would. We had left a note at the lodge door telling where we had gone. I couldn't fly the Super Cub so I would have had to wait there at the lake by the plane if they weren't with me—wait and wait—.

Another one of my jobs as a bush pilot's wife was driving the new Chrysler station wagon to go to Anchorage for grocery supplies, meeting the clients on their arrival at Gulkana Air Field and returning them after their hunts. Bud had all the flying to do but I liked this job. Our hunting business was getting busier and we were booking more clients, that meant more guides and assistant guides. I even had a helper in the kitchen at times during a busy hunting season.

The real challenge for me was on the Nabesna Road. The four wheel drive Jeep or the pickup could cross those creeks that were running across the road (no bridges.) After rains and in the spring when melting snows filled the creeks and water ran deep across the road I often had to lay planks across a creek. Planks two feet wide and long enough to reach across to shallower ground were left alongside the road just for these needs. I would put my hip-boots on and check for the shallowest crossing. When driving the station wagon it meant putting a plank in front of each front wheel and staying on the plank until I had crossed. Only once did I slide off on a back wheel and I had to put a "Handy-Man" jack under the wheel then drive out to solid ground. Bud would usually be waiting for me at Long Lake. If I didn't show up when he thought I should he'd fly over to see if I had a problem, then walk down the road to help me. I could change a tire or do most things that it took to get running again.

The variety of personnel that one meets on these trips keeps conversations lively and interesting. They are all successful business men and not often exposed to capable females who can pretty much do all the things they expect only a man to do. I am always amused at the reaction from one or more of them when they see so much water running across the road and wonder if they are expected to get out and wade across or help me. I assure them everything is under control but talking this over among themselves they sound doubtful. Then if Bud flies over about then and I tell them even if I do get stuck he will walk down to meet us, they act real relieved. The majority of the time I am across and driving down the road when I meet Bud coming. They will nearly always tell him what a lucky guy he is to have a helper like me. I agree of course.

I enjoy my passengers reaction to the spectacular view of our mountains as we drive up the road. If one of the men has booked a sheep hunt it's not unusual to hear him say he didn't know our sheep hills were that high and would ask if the big rams were clear to the top. We watch a bull moose with massive antlers, standing in the middle of the road, then disappears into the trees with those huge antlers held back over his shoulders.

I stop alongside the road where we saw him last but he is gone. That never fails to give a hunter a thrill, especially if a wolf, or maybe a grizzly bear, lopes across the road. That gets them excited and gives them something to look forward to and talk about for the rest of the day.

There are times I find myself in a position where I have to make a decision right there on the spot. Mostly I have used good judgement but I came close to making the wrong decision one day when I drove to Gulkana Airfield to meet a Cordova Airlines plane. We had two clients booked for a fifteen day hunt for Dall rams, moose and a caribou. In their correspondence one man indicated he was paying for both men to hunt and also a photographer he was bringing along. They wanted time for a fishing trip and would pay extra if their time went over the fifteen days. These are the type of clients an outfitter needs in this business. In the majority of correspondence a prospective client will give his age and some background. These fellows had not, plus they turned out to be younger than I had expected.

I arrived at the airport a bit early and, as usual, the plane was late. I was visiting with another outfitter's wife who also had clients to meet. Then while the plane was landing I drove the station wagon closer to where the passengers would debark. It's always a fun time to watch the passengers as they come down the steps and onto the ramp I try to spot which of the men will be mine to take back with me. Other outfitters are waiting and it's easy to pick out the guys who are going on a hunt. They don't wear a business suite and at that time they could carry their rifle on the plane with them.

The captain and copilot got out first and were standing at the door as three men came down the steps. They were arguing with the stewardess and the captain is telling them something and trying to get them out of the way so the other passengers can exit. One man has a professional looking camera around his neck. I am far enough away that I can't hear what they are saying but it's obvious those men are drunk and have no intention of letting the plane leave unless?…Unless what?

I backed the station wagon farther away and parked it behind the others waiting so these fellows wouldn't see me. I had to decide how to handle this because I know Bud Conkle wouldn't fly them over to Tanada as drunk as all three of them were. I just about had made up my mind to drive a few miles back to the nearest motel and book a room and leave them there until morning. That however would create a problem too. Because I would have to drive back to where Bud would be waiting and fly over to the lodge, there was no one there to fix dinner for the other men there. Bud would then have to fly me back out in the morning and he had other flying to do.

All this went through my thoughts and just as I started up the engine to leave, two very friendly looking young men walked up along side and asked if I was Mrs. Bud Conkle? They and the photographer with them were our clients. We didn't wait to see who the lucky outfitter was who was waiting for his hunters who were also bringing a photographer with them. My hunters told me the fuss between those hunters and the captain was that the stewardess had taken their case of whiskey away from them and they were not leaving until they got it back!

I could have got myself behind the eight ball by jumping to conclusions that time.

Bud and LeNora.

Chapter Six

Other Enjoyable Tasks

The outfitter's wife is often called upon to be den mother to some of the men who come to hunt, or sometimes to guide, assistant guides, the boys who are hired as packers or to animals and birds who need a bandage or more detailed doctoring. Where did she learn such a variety of helpful information. I'd be willing to say she just uses her own good judgment.

Two medical doctors arrived back in base camp with very badly blistered feet. They had climbed the sheep hills with climbing boots that were not well broken in. I took one look at those blistered feet and put a basin of hot water and epsom salt down with orders to soak their feet. "Oh, we have salve in our gear at our tent," one of the doctors informed me. "This works best," I said. "Who is the doctor here?" he asked. "I am. Now put your blistered feet in this hot epsom salt water and stay right where you are," I said.

They did and complained the water was too hot but I informed them it wasn't going to feel hot very long and when I'd feel it was cooling I'd add more hot water. About ten minutes and they agreed it did feel good. The next morning they were ready to go again and couldn't believe how well it worked. That treatment toughens the feet I told them and they had to admit it worked better than the salve they would have used, that only soothed the blisters.

Epsom salts was something we used and always had in our camps. More than a few blistered feet have been cured with this method. I felt smug letting two doctors think I knew something they didn't.

One year during hunting season a pilot set two resident sheep hunters out on a high lake in the mountains above Tanada

Lake. When he was due back to fly them back out to their car on the highway, a storm kept all pilots grounded for three days. Two Air Force captains from Eielson Air Force Base (near Fairbanks) had taken their own groceries for what was to be the length of their hunt. Knowing no airplane would be in to fly them out in this bad weather, they walked out to Tanada Lake. They had seen the lay of the land when flying in to their camp and had the lodge spotted. Bud heard a couple of rifle shots and spotted them at the head of the lake and went to get them with the motor boat. They were tired, hungry, cold, and dirty. They were fairly young but their age was hard to judge with their faces so dirty from smoke of a camp fire. I couldn't help but laugh at their bright eyes looking out from the frosted fur that lined their parka hoods that made a circle around their faces. They both looked like bright eyed animals peeking out from a fur lined face.

I mothered them like sons of my own. A hot meal, with heated water for a hot bath, a change of dry clothes and when they emerged they looked like two good looking thirty-year-old men instead of two ugly ducklings. Everyone, including his buddy, had a good laugh at the one guy dressed in my jeans and sweater. Bud's clothes fit the other one pretty tightly. He could barely button them. The way they laughed at him wearing bib overalls I'm sure it wasn't what he normally wore. They were grateful and they were fun. Bud was grounded also, and we had two hunters waiting to be flown out to their camps and those two men kept us entertained with flying stories as well as some of the funny or tough experiences during their military careers. They were with us for two days before their pilot could come to get them. Their pilot was Art Smith, a pilot who was always a fun person to have stop over when flying in our area. We knew him well from the various times he was weathered in here while trying to get up to one of the high lakes that was fogged in.

There were times I mended a client's clothes if he tore a hole some place important and didn't have a change. I patched jeans, sewed on buttons, for the boys helping us during hunting season; especially when they had been climbing or going through thick brush. Also I impressed one of our clients with a birthday cake. His hunting buddies told me it was his birthday. Earlier he had shot a real trophy caribou bull. A friend was helping me in the kitchen and we made a cake big enough to feed the crew and clients and we did a fancy job of decorating it with an improvised small animal we found in Colin's toy box. We put big antlers on it made from thin sticks. The top of the cake was covered with short bushes loaded with blue berries and scattered red berries. We sure were on that man's "best friend" list. He said he had never had a birthday cake since he had been married. He sure wasn't an underprivileged business man. Wondering what his wife was like, I decided he was always away from home on business or a hunt on his birthday.

I could always find time to take care of orphaned baby rabbits, feeding them with an eye dropper. There was an orphan baby duck I kept in a box, babied and fed until it was ready to swim away with a mama duck and her brood. It joined them like it belonged there. We had a gull with a broken wing I fed it mosquitoes and flies. I had to find time to catch food and put on the water so it would gobble them up. I never found anything else it would eat that would have been a lot more convenient to feed it. It was running around in the house and following me every where I went. It kept picking the bandage off I had put on to hold the wounded wing. It dragged the wing and didn't seem to be healing. I thought it would enjoy a day out doors on the water, I carried it down to the lake and constructed a floating corral surrounding the plane's pontoons so it couldn't swim away. Something called me back to the cabin and after awhile I remembered the bird and went back to see how he was faring. I don't know how he managed to get turned over on his back, but there it was floating. It had drowned. When you have these animals or birds very long they get to be real pets and it's sad to lose them. I am always hoping to heal them and return them to the wild. One day while driving I found a baby owl in the middle of the highway as I was returning from Glennallen. I presumed that an antenna from a passing car had hit it and spun it around and it fell to the middle of the road. Its wing wasn't broken but it couldn't fly. It was ready to fight me when I stopped to see why it was just sitting there rather stunned. I put my coat over it and carried it to the station wagon. It stayed quiet without trying to get out of the coat. Back home I put it in a rabbit hutch we had and for a week I'd mix raw hamburger with egg and feed it out of my hand. This bird didn't have a broken wing but dragged the injured wing around when it moved in its cage. I would put food near by, but to no avail, it wouldn't eat. If I held the food it would make an attempt to eat, if I put food in my open hand the owl gobbled it up. It was so big I had a time convincing myself it was still a very young owl. About ten days after I brought it home I'd take it out of the cage and lift it up and down trying to convince it to try to fly. It would only fly a short distance and land. When I'd reach to pick it up it would turn on its back with claws reaching up to grab me. I'd tell it that it was an ungrateful owl and put it back in the cage. We had it so long that it was quite a pet. I took it out of the cage one day to let it fly and Colin asked to hold it. I set it on his arm and it promptly flew away. The last we saw of our baby owl was when it sailed away off into the distance and over the tree tops, never returning to eat the food set out on top of its cage.

One day Colin had an accident in his little green skiff. He has been able to run the motor on the fourteen-foot AlumaCraft boat since he was a four-year-old. This day I was busy in the kitchen and heard him bring the boat to the dock, shut the motor off, but I didn't see him take the smaller wooden skiff out. He is never allowed on the lake without his life jacket. His dad had also advised him not to put the unbalanced metal thirty-five-gallon barrel in the skiff, because it made the skiff unstable. Colin didn't heed that advice. This day he planned to paddle along close to shore. He had put his hip boots on and (for some unusual reason), had left his life jacket on the shore. I would often look out a window to see what he is doing. This day I was expecting him to come up to the cabin after he tied up the boat. I heard a desperate yell and dropped what I was doing and ran down to the dock. He was in the water, out from shore where it was deep, his skiff was floating away from him. Without hesitating I kicked my shoes off and swam out to pull him back to shore. The lake water was always too cold for him to learn to swim. I never noticed how cold it was until we were back on shore. He had lost his balance when a wave hit the skiff he then fell over the barrel and into the water. His hip boots quickly filled with water, he thought he could wade back to shore! That was a lesson he would remember. I was wondering what would have happened to him if I had been in the other room with any obstructing noise. What if I hadn't heard him yell? He only yelled that one time before he went under, and then bobbed up. I was praying he'd stay afloat until I could get to him. It was normal for Bud to be gone during these types of emergencies, not due back until late or even until the next day. Instances like that make a person realize just how isolated they are and without communications of any kind. I am not the only woman in situations like this, perhaps we feel equipped to rise to 'the calling' for all these out of the normal happenings that we are called upon to handle.

There was another time when Bud was away flying and not due back until morning, that could have ended up differently than it did. The last of the fishing customers were gone, the dinner dishes washed, Colin and I took the motor boat to go fishing. It was a lovely warm evening and not a ripple on the water. We planned to slow row and not disturb the silent evening with the shattering sounds of an outboard boat motor. Colin was at the oars, and I no more than got my line as far out behind us as I wanted it when I caught a fish that was full of fight. Apparently this one had been close to the boat dock and had been eating the guts tossed into the lake where those fisherman had cleaned their grayling before they left. I started reeling in and when that lake trout got close enough to the boat and I could see how big it was, it dove under the boat. "Oh, did you see that fish? It's big! I have never caught one that big. We sure don't want this one to get away." I excitedly handled the pole trying to turn the fish but had to let out more line. When I'd bring it close to the boat I'd hold the line taut. Colin tried to get it into the net but it would flip and splash away. On the third try the handle of the net fell off. He tried to lean over the edge and put both arms around the fish and haul it into the boat but it was too slippery. I handed Colin the pole and when he got that big mouth up close I reached down inside its open mouth thinking I'd pull it in the boat. It clamped down on my hand and I had to force its jaws open to release my bloody hand. Blood was running down my hand but I didn't let it bother me. I wanted to get that fish in the boat. I guess we both were too excited to note how long we had battled that trout. On one last desperate try, he reached down and put his arms around that monster and landed it. I'm sure It was as tired as we were by then.

Our little dog Pedro was with us in the boat and without using good judgment, Colin and I both would be leaning over the edge of the low side, the dog also had to watch, tipping the boat far enough to ship water. As I thought about it later, I was thankful the lake was calm because had there been waves I'm sure the boat would have swamped and dumped all three of us into the lake far away from shore. I am not sure who all would have survived. We were so excited trying to bring that big fish into the boat we didn't give any thought to what might be happening. When we were back on shore that lake trout weighed twenty-nine pounds. The biggest one taken out of Tanada Lake as of yet.

When Bud returned just at dusk (about 11:30 PM), Colin and I were leading our trophy, on a heavy line back and forth in shallow water near shore to keep it alive. I wanted to have it mounted because it was my only trophy. I had shot a caribou bull one time thinking I wanted to be a hunter also but Bud didn't make himself popular with me when he gave those antlers to a hunter who wanted them. Just a coincidence that Colin had stepped on a rusty nail earlier in the day and I had been having him soak his foot in hot epsom salt water. When Bud returned we thought it best we fly out to the hospital and have the doctor there look at it because it was swelling and looked angry. About midnight we landed on Grizzly Lake close to the Tok highway. Fred and Jean Freidricks hadn't gone to bed yet and put us up in one of their cabins. The next day Jean drove us to the hospital where Colin was treated with no further complications.

I didn't get off without a scolding about not using good judgment in taking a chance on sinking the boat out from under the three of us. "How would I have felt on returning home and only the green wooden boat gone from the dock and you three not here? Why didn't you take the AlumaCraft? The sides on it are high and it's more stable," he scolded. "Would a twenty-nine-pound fish have been worth it?"

After the scolding I had given Colin about his dunking while out in the skiff, I didn't return the comment I thought would be appropriate at this time. I wanted to remind him about that time he and I were in that same low sided boat and planning to bring some tools back from across the lake. I took my fishing pole and was trolling with my favorite big 'Dare Devil' lure. I was starting to reel the line in and alongside the boat a big lake trout followed it and startled me. I yelled at Bud to cut the motor. He saw it also when it nudged the shiny lure, missing the hooks, then dove. We spent most of that day trying to lure it back, knowing if it got hooked we'd surely have stayed with it trying to get it into the boat or leading it to shore and knowing how bad we both wanted to catch it, we could well have been excited and sunk that unstable boat. Some of our clients have also been excited about having a huge lake trout follow their lures but wouldn't bite. Yes, I admit I was too interested in getting my big fish and not using good judgment.

My lake trout was put into Jean's freezer at Grizzly lake, our neighbor on the highway, then sent out to a taxidermist to be mounted life size. What an opportunity to have it taken care of, because otherwise it surely would have spoiled. It was displayed in the trophy room at Tanada Lake until it was moved to Eagle Trail Ranch a few years later.

Is there ever a remedy for worry for a wife or mother at home waiting? My remedy is simply a prayer for their safety. Then I wait and wait, look out a window to the lake, all the while listening for that familiar sound of the returning Super Cub, or the motor boat if the lake is moving with angry waves in a sudden storm that frequents big lakes and comes up swiftly when we are unprepared. There were times when I watched from the lookout on the hill as a boat was caught out in the wide bay when the winds suddenly came up strong and the occupants of the boat were desperately trying to make it back to the safe haven of shore. It seems every summer there are drownings in a big lake due to sudden storms and rough water and if I could help it, I surely didn't want this to happen on Tanada Lake.

A long day of worried time for me was watching my two macho men crossing the lake in high waves. From my vantage place on Look-Out hill, with the binoculars, I could uneasily watch as they crossed the mile-wide lake to the opposite side, the boat bouncing in the chop as its square nose moved slowly in the direction they were heading and with Bud expertly quartering into each wave they slowly made smoother water. They followed the far shore line and rounded a curve and out of my sight. I was expecting any one of those high waves to swamp their boat. Both were wearing rain coats and Colin had his hood clear down covering his face, Bud wore his cap without the hood covering it. Watching them leave the dock I would wonder if this would be the picture I'd best remember.

It had rained all night and was still raining but Bud wanted to go out to the lower end of the lake with the boat, park it and walk a couple miles across the tundra where he had left the weasel. He had to take a part to repair it and then would drive it back and pick up the boat and haul it back to Saw Mill creek. He would leave the weasel sit there until he could install the new track and have it ready for hunting season. Bud and Colin had taken a lunch and said they would catch a fish to cook it over a camp fire for dinner if they got hungry because it would take all day and perhaps be late before they would signal me they were back. Our signals were a fire on shore at Saw Mill creek and I'd be back up on my lookout hill to watch them cross and hoping and praying the lake was calm. It was. "Why take chances like you do and with our son along," I asked him. "You were impatient to get going regardless of the weather and rough water and that unstable boat in such high waves."

"He wanted to go with me, and he just as well learn that nothing in the life style we live here is going to be easy. I wasn't taking any chances. I knew I could handle it," was his answer.

"I wanted to go and Daddy said I could if I didn't complain," was Colin's input.

"He wasn't too enthused about getting dumped in the lake but he kept his head under the hood of his rain coat until we are across and in smoother water. He helped to drive the weasel and gives out constant advice," Bud added.

I need not have worried. He was in safe hands.

Chapter Seven

Eagle Ranch Trail

As if we didn't already have enough work and business at Tanada Lake, Bud came in one day after returning from the sheep hills, to inform me he was getting tired of the competition from some of the Anchorage based pilot-guides crowding the areas where he had his camps and hunters set out. He was seriously thinking of moving over into the Nutzotin Range, a branch of the Wrangells, where he had been flying his

Bud plowing snow on the mile of road from the Tok Highway to Eagle Trail Ranch.

moose and bear hunters the past two seasons. This particular day had him about as upset as I have ever seen him. Two Super Cubs flying together had deliberately buzzed the rams away from his hunters. Those two clients camps were on a lake at the base of the mountain they had climbed and almost reached the Dall rams they would shoot. Bud had his special descriptive words to describe the unethical pilots who over booked clients and were not particular where they set them out to hunt, even if there were other hunters in the same area. Bud was considered a fair chase guide and outfitter. He knew who those pilots were but left them for the Fish and Game agents to control.

"Every year it's getting harder and harder for my clients to get good trophies the way those pilots wholesale the game" he said.

After twenty years of hunting in the Wrangells, Bud Conkle informs me he is planning to buy horses and set up his hunting camps on the small lake close to the Snag River at the base of the Nutzotin mountain. I had no idea he had been so seriously thinking about this, as well as buying horses to use. I also had to give this some thought. He had grown up with horses and before he went to the Service he had worked as a hunting guide for outfitters who used pack and saddle horses.

"Where will you get horses and where will we keep them," I wanted to know, starting to think about a corral on this five acres with all the clearing involved as well as how he planned to feed them.

"I'll go to Canada to buy horses, then we'll apply for a hundred-sixty-acres for a homestead on Cobb Lake. We'll sell this five acres and the lodge and move down there as soon as we get a cabin to live in.

We had often flown from Tanada Lake and landed on Cobb Lake, anchored the airplane, hiked up the low hill a half mile to the Tok highway, and Bud had frequently mentioned this would be an ideal place for a homestead, and he should apply while he still had his three years left on his application time for his military G.I. homestead act, which was enough time to improve the land and get a title. It was an ideal base for float planes and he had it all figured out where a landing strip could be built for wheel landings. Cobb Lake had ample room for larger planes as well as Super Cubs.

I was eager to see the area he had told me about when he first took hunters to the Nutzotin Range. He had to make extra trips with the plane that was required to take two hunters and a camp for a week. It was just too far away for all the flying involved unless Bud flew one hunter there for an overnight camp and back the next day if he had his moose or a bear. Then it was extra flying to get the meat and hide or horns out.

Bud wanted to fly me over there hoping to sell me on the advantage of outfitting with horses in this remote country. He had noted the variety of game and with no evidence of any one else hunting there. The lake was close to canyons with creeks running in and located at the base of sheep hills.

We planned a day in late June after the ice would be gone from the lake there and the Super Cub was changed from skis to floats. The ice didn't leave Tanada Lake until the end of June but there was open water at the lower end to make the change and take off with the load we'd have. It was an exciting day we chose for the flight. Bud had pointed out on the map the route we'd fly from Tanada Lake. We left early while the sun was still a low ball in the sky, pink edged clouds moved slowly across the pale sky. We flew low over a scattered bunch of caribou on the top of the round mountain across the lake from the lodge, on across the Nabesna road then the Nabesna river with a low overfly of the old abandoned Indian village near the river, then eastward alongside snow capped mountains which my pilot informed me was the Nutzotin range. Bud circled a small pond— at least it looked like a pond to me in comparison to Tanada Lake—with small ripples on the water created by a soft breeze. The pontoons touched lightly on the water and taxiing across to the far shore he cut the motor and the cub settled on Wolf Lake. Bud had named this lake for the wolves in the area that serenaded the hunters during their September hunt.

We had taken camping equipment for an over night stay, giving us a day to climb one of the lower hills and explore an inviting canyon near our camp. Returning late from an adventurous day, a nipping wind with threatening rain hurried us back to camp. Fresh grizzly tracks overlaid our tracks in the mud close to where we left the shore line. Just a curious bear, Bud surmised, because it didn't investigate our camp. As we walked along the shore both ways Bud pointed out the abundance of feed for horses that was growing around the lake. He made it a point to note the pea-vine and wild grasses growing along the creek which made for excellent horse feed.

Smoke from our camp fire floated away on a light summer

breeze as we rested our tired bodies by the warm fire, talking and planning the move. We talked of and about selling Tanada Lake Lodge. Yes, I agreed with Bud's reasoning about setting up a hunting camp here.

The fluorescent changing colors on the purple foot hills, as the sun was slowly leaving beyond a mountain, reflected in the windshield of the cub riding at anchor close by. A rude wind arose suddenly untidied the smoke, blowing it back in our faces and we got into our sleeping bags comfortable in the decision we have made. I went to sleep with the soothing lullaby of the slap-slapping of water against the aluminum pontoons.

It had been a long time since I had hiked and climbed with my pilot-guide husband in gorgeous wilderness, for me, this was a very enjoyable and romantic trip.

With Bud's normal 'get-with-it' way of getting things done, it didn't take him long to write up an add for the sale of Tanada Lake Lodge. I had to leave whatever I was doing to type up the ad and get it ready for the mail. Reading it over he made a remark that to me was a real amusing comment. "Gee, this place sounds like an ideal place where I'd like to buy and run a big game hunting business."

"Oh yeh!" Shall we keep it ? The letter isn't mailed yet," was my comment with a noticeable smirk in my voice and a smug grin on my face.

Thomas Dean, a BLM manager for the North Slope stationed in Fairbanks, bought Tanada Lake Lodge before we had time to change our minds. So now we start all over, just in different locations.

Bud located a second hand Caterpillar and after many dedicated hours of rebuilding it, he went to work with real enthusiasm clearing the twenty acres for the 160 acre homestead he had applied for. I was still busy at the lodge because we were still getting fishing customers. Bud would take time from his land clearing project to fly people in who didn't have their own airplanes. The new owner wouldn't be in a position to take over until late fall. I informed my husband that no way was I going to spend a winter in a tent like we did those first two years when we started at Tanada Lake. "I'll stay here and cook for Tom Dean's customers unless we have a cabin to live in. Do you remember me telling you I'd go to Alaska with you if you'd promise we'd have a log cabin with a stone fireplace? We had the log cabin without a fireplace so I still plan to have a log cabin with a stone fireplace eventually and it will be on that land."

A week later Bud flew some fishermen in who would need a rented boat and a cabin with their meals.

Another one of my duties was keeping the boat motors fueled unless Bud had time when he was there. This trip he was too busy telling me about the two frame cabins he heard were for sale and he had bought them. He explained that they were built in such a way they would fit together for two rooms. First he would have to clear land by the lake where they would be placed and would have to make a wider trail from the highway down there, but this would have to wait until the ground was frozen because too much of the trail was swamp.

A busy hunting season took preference over all other activi-

LeNora feeding horses.

ties and it was into November before Bud could clear brush for an improvised road that followed an old trail from the highway to Cobb Lake, a mile and a half. With the help of two friends and a borrowed sled, with the bulldozer to tow the sled, he skidded two 10'14' cabins, one at a time, to the clearing. Colin at that time was boarding in Valdez for the school term with our friends, Max and Betty Wells and their large family.

By the time I had everything packed we'd be moving to our new home, Bud had attached the two cabins together having a hallway between, stoves in place and ready to move into. We drove to Valdez to bring Colin home for our first Christmas in our new home. It wasn't exactly a luxurious modern home but we were accustomed to doing without running water, outhouse with a warm seat in winter and all those other modern bush inventory. We did have electricity within the year when a generator was added to our conveniences.

Two wood stoves didn't keep us very warm, but we kept warm by getting wood from the surrounding area and cutting it up. The man who built the cabins told Bud they were insulated for deep, cold winters in mind. It was into the next winter when we discovered there were squirrel families also living in close proximity that were insulating their homes with the corn-husks that Cheechako man had used for our cabin insulation. Our squirrel neighbors loved it.

All three of us put in long hours all summer, then winter as long as daylight and temperatures allowed. Keeping a wood supply consumed much of our time before cold weather set in and we'd had no time to re-insulate so most of our heat went out the sides and ceiling. Not much improvement over a tent. I was happy when summer came.

Bud was taking brown bear clients to the Alaska Peninsula on fifteen day hunts in March now. When he returned he left for Canada to haul home the horses he had bought from an outfitter in the Yukon. He built side boards on our two ton truck and could haul four horses and the man he bought them from would haul the remaining six. Bud had a fairly large pole corral finished before he left. These were all considered range horses and didn't need a barn. He would learn which two or more horses to keep in the corral and then the others would stay around fairly close. We had a load of hay delivered and would also feed them oats, at feeding time they would all be waiting. We still spent a lot of time going after horses and especially keeping them off the highway where they liked to stand on the warm pavement. This added project didn't allow time for home improvement. I wasn't doing any entertainment so the neglected housework didn't disturb my tendency for neatness.

A driveable road from the highway to the cabin was another year or two in the future. The station wagon and truck had to be parked a short distance off the highway in a clearing Bud had bulldozed. We were back packing again. Now instead of seven miles of swampy tundra humps we had a mile and a half of gooey clay to traipse across when it was raining. Everything from the car had to be back packed all summer unless on a frozen trail then Bud used the bulldozer to pull a sled he made. We had a variety of furniture, new or second hand, to haul after each trip to Anchorage, as well as cases of canned food. One trip the sled tipped over and spilled everything. I had muddy everything to clean, including a box of my books. I had books to read with muddy covers and muddy torn pages to decipher.

To qualify for the land, Bud cleared 20 acres of stunted northern black spruce and willows, then pushed them into berm piles that had to be burned so oats could be planted. It was pretty much Colin and my job to keep those piles burning. Even with the smoke from the burning piles the mosquitoes were fierce. Stirring up the muskeg and vegetation with the bulldozer routed out the biggest and fiercest of those Alaska pests. When disturbed they were inclined to resent the intrusion. They took every opportunity to get even. We used a lot of repellant and spray and moved fast to gain entrance through a screen door without letting a horde in with us. Bud took a fiendish pleasure in standing inside the screens and pulling the "snout straws" off from the ones that poked their straws through the screen trying to reach his hand. He didn't let their bites bother him and seldom used a repellant, he just scratched their itchy bites into submission. All those years at Tanada Lake there weren't many mosquitoes on the hillside where the lodge was located so we had pretty much forgotten how determined they were to share our blood.

We named this new homesteaded land EAGLE TRAIL RANCH because the original Eagle Trail (a trail blazed for a telegraph line starting from Valdez and ending at Eagle, Alaska) following along the eastern shore of Cobb Lake. A half a mile of it was included within the survey of our land. Horses are associated with ranches so we felt the name appropriate. This historic trail was built in the early 1900s when Fort Egbert was an active military base, Captain Billy Mitchell, who later became a champion of air power, was in charge. I was impressed with all that early history and especially when we had met some of those old-timers who had worked on that trail when it was being built.

I had a lot of adjusting to make from what had become a comfortable home at Tanada Lake to a new home at Eagle Trail

Wolf Lake with Mother Nature Peaks.

Ranch. When the Northern Lights blazoned across the sky in all their colorful glory, changing colors, they seemed to send me a message that they are here as well as at Tanada Lake. From the bedroom window I could see them, I would go outside to watch and it was like an old friend stopping by to say hello.

We kept the horses at the ranch part of the summer in order to get acquainted with them and for them to know they belonged here. The Copper River was a quarter of a mile beyond the lake and our property. There was good horse feed on the sand bars. When we were not planning to ride them we'd take them down an old game trail to the river and turn them loose. They were content to stay there until it was time to bring them back home then haul them over to hunting country. Our neighbor, Doc Taylor at Grizzly Lake would come with his truck and horse trailer and help load and haul them from the ranch over to where they would be unloaded near the Canada border.

Bud had two horse wranglers hired for the season and each would ride one of the saddle horses. Lead a pack horse and the rest would be loose, but would follow. A friend had volunteered to ride in with them on that first trip and every one got a real workout on the old dim lit trail they followed traversing a ridge to the Chisana river. There were many downed trees that had to be chopped through for the horses to traverse, with the Chisana River yet to cross in two different places then follow the river to the base of the mountain on a game trail to Wolf Lake. It would take them four days, camping overnight staking some of the horses and hobbling the others. Always there was one or more of their charges that wanted to linger behind to graze or even return to where they started. Bud flew over them twice a day to follow their progress to be sure they were following the right directions. If they were held up waiting, or looking for a missing horse, he'd locate it, circle to let the boys know where it was, then stay in the area until they were on their way again. It was two years before we blazed a clear trail for the horses and their wranglers to follow the river, to Wolf Lake. Always major undertaking to get the horses to hunting country and back out to the highway when hunting season was over.

It had been my job to pack lunches and camp groceries for the three wranglers and their estimated three day trip. Bud would make an airdrop if they signaled they were out of food. Some of the later years it took five days getting the horses to hunting country. My other job, and I liked this one, was driving our new Chrysler station wagon to Anchorage for the cased groceries that had to last all through hunting season at Wolf Lake. I would load everything that automobile would hold as it would be my last chance to go to a wholesale grocery store this season. I had as many as eight men to feed, for those ten day hunts—that meant four assistant guides and two (sometimes three) wranglers and a very busy pilot. With all the wild meat we had in camp and my past years of experience in cooking it, I kept them well fed even with home made bread and blueberry pies. I never heard any complaints from anyone.

When the fall hunts were over at Wolf Lake it was my responsibility to drive the clients to the Gulkana Airfield to catch their connecting flights home from Anchorage. This let me be the first one flown out to the highway leaving the crew to clean up the kitchen and close the camp for the winter while Bud had all the flying to do. I'd be the first back at the ranch to open the cabin, start the fires and start putting things away. Then when the horses and airplane were back to Eagle Trail Ranch it was time for Bud to prepare for the brown bear hunts on the Alaska Peninsula. The clients trophies had to be taken to the taxidermist in Anchorage or prepared for shipping. The pontoons had to be taken off the Super Cub and wheels (the big tundra tires) mounted, tents and camping gear for fifteen days, (more often twenty) mended and packed. We all worked in high gear. There was always a tent to be mended and sleeping bags aired, I'd take care of these while Bud had full responsibility of the airplane.

A major worry of pilots who were forced to leave their airplanes on isolated airstrips or lakes, was to be out of sight of the plane and then have a bear come along and tear it up. They are especially careful when hauling meat or fish to keep all odors and blood cleaned up. There have been airplanes torn up without any excuse by a bear that just happened along. A case in point; a grizzly bear ripped the fabric from both sides of our Super Cub while it was parked in front of the garage, loaded and ready to fly to the Peninsula for the hunts.

"The only excuse that bear had was to get revenge for all his relatives I let my clients collect," Bud said, as he sorted through the hunting gear that was scattered in the snow all around the plane, while picking out what was still usable. While he was loosening bolts to take the wings off, he was talking to that departed bear and I doubt if any bear had ever been called so many uncomplimentary names. He dispatched me to go to the neighbors to get help in getting the wings and fuselage into the garage in the event the bear returned to finish the ripping job or eat the can of food it had bitten into—but left uneaten. That bear could not have possibly chosen a more inconvenient time to tear up the plane, one more day and the plane would have been gone from here. After the airplane was safe in the garage I asked him what about me? What if it comes back and wants in the house?

"Shoot it. Keep your gun loaded and be sure to hit it in a vital spot like I have always instructed you. You don't need a wounded bear around while I am gone." That was his parting answer when he left for the two week hunt in mid October without his own airplane, hoping to lease one on such short notice, as it is important to use two planes for transportation for

A grizzly bear tore up the Super Cub setting in front of the garage at Eagle Trail Ranch.

the amount of hunters booked. It had start snowing the evening before Bud was to leave, but he planned to leave at daylight anyway. I had just finished the new wing covers that pilots faithfully use to protect wings from snow and ice. Bud had, that very afternoon put them on, he wanted to take them with him on the hunt. He wasn't sure I could have them finished in time. I'd have been real mad too if that grizz' had torn them up, but they were left intact.

I spent a few uneasy days watching for that bear to come

back. It didn't but a real snow storm did. It started snowing heavier on the day Bud left but I was still able to drive the pickup out on our road without having to plow snow if need be. Five days later the snow was five feet deep! Too deep and wet even for our snowmobile to make it out to the highway for the mail or otherwise.

Colin was home and enrolled in a correspondence school. I was the teacher and that took much of our day. Colin was a lot of help but not for the total job of feeding thirteen horses oats and hay every morning. They were waiting at the corral every morning regardless of the deep snow. The book work (after a busy hunting season) took care of the rest of my day. On the sixth day two neighbor boys brought in the mail and to check on us to see how we were coping. Their snowmachines were later models and more powerful than ours, still they spent much of their time getting unstuck. Their visit was very much appreciated. It seems the men were just home from the brown bear hunts when it was time for them to leave for the polar bear hunts. Bud and his partner, Cleo McMahan, hunted out from Barrow, Alaska in the months of February and March. Many of the polar bear hunting pilot-guides hunted out from Kotzebue. They hunted together on what was called the buddy-system. Two Super Cubs flying tandem as a safety factor while one airplane carried the hunter the other plane flew cover. When the pilots were on this type of hunt they usually had access to a telephone, and would call home on arrival and when departing so the women waiting at home didn't have the responsibility of their flight plans. That didn't mean when they left for home they would show up on schedule. They could leave Barrow or Kotzebue in good weather but fly into whiteouts or storms, then be forced to sit out the weather someplace where they have no way of sending word home. They are well prepared and experienced for these emergencies and their wives, waiting at home, know this. Still they wait and hope. Like most wives, I trusted they'd show up sooner or later. Regardless (when too long overdue), one wonders. There was the time Bud and Cleo had left Barrow in good weather but spent a few days camped on a lake in a whiteout. They were comfortable but no one knew they were setting out the weather. It could have been totally different if one or the other plane had crashed during a whiteout landing when they couldn't see above or below them.

Cleo McMahan's wife, Daphne, and I had ways of contacting each other to find if there was any late news from our husbands. She was home with four kids and it was always a comfort to both of us at any time we had a chance to meet and visit awhile. She was a busy lady with those active children, driving them to all the various school activities in which they were involved.

I well remember the one year when Bud and Cleo had the two polar bear clients booked for a brown bear hunt soon as their Arctic hunt was completed. Weather held them some place along their way home. When we eventually heard from our men it was via phone call from Fairbanks. My message was delivered to me from a neighbor by telephone, saying I was to bring the wheels and all pertinent wheel changing gear needed, then meet him at Paxson Lake the next day. Daphne had the same message from Cleo. No matter what it involved it was for us to deliver the request, so we met our husbands at Paxson Lake. While they helped each other with the change over from skis to the wheels, we now found our selves with time on our hands and could catch up on some of their news. Then they kissed us a mighty short good bye and were off into the air and on their way. It would be fifteen days or more before they would be back home.

Back at the ranch the work went on, but there was more than enough work left for him to catch up with when he returned, even with the newly hired ranch hand, Bob Nelson. He was a young man who came to work for us and stayed three years until he left to return to college.

The first summer he was with us a cow moose spent a lot of time around the ranch and thought it her privilege to share the hay with the horses. For some unusual reason she would make a run at Bob if he went out to toss hay, yet Bud could yell at her and she would leave. When Bud would unload hay from the truck into the corral the cow would jump the fence and after eating as much as she wanted she'd climb on top of the hay to have a nap scattering hay in all directions. If that wasn't brazen enough she resented anyone trying to chase her out of the corral. She had simply moved in. She especially resented

Bob even walking past her, with ears back she'd run at the fence like she was intending to jump it. It would take a fool, or maybe a person using poor judgment, to argue with a mad cow moose. Their front hooves are as dangerous as grizzly bear claws. Bob had to wait for me to drive the car past her and block her view to rescue him for lunch or whatever.

She made a run at Colin one day but he was in the front door by the time she was over the fence. "I am going to get rid of the damn cow," he said as he picked up the .30-06 rifle and headed back out the door.

"Heavens no! Don't shoot her. She is carrying a calf unless that belly is full of hay," I yelled at him.

His intention was only to shoot over her back to scare her but she went back to pawing hay from the pile to the ground and ignored the loud shots. Okay, I'll try something else. "Oh, I know," he said and started out the door with the chain saw!

I grabbed the camera and started up the station wagon and pulled it up close to the fence with the door opened, planning to get a movie of the cow chasing Colin, leaving the door open so he could jump in. When he started the chain saw she went over the fence, so I didn't get the picture I wanted.

The next day when the cow moose was back. Colin once again took the chain saw out to the corral and started it and again she went over the fence into the trees. That was the way to get rid of her. A few days later Colin was in the outhouse with the door open. It faced away from the house and on a well worn trail. This day Bud walked out the cabin door just in time to see that cow come jumping and snorting down the trail. Bud yelled at Colin to stay inside. That cow had her ears back and she was mad about something. She hit the back of the outhouse with both front feet then again went jumping down the trail and disappeared. We never saw her again but often wondered what had her so stirred up. It's possible she may have lost her calf. This was early June and the moose cows would drop their calves about this time or in late May. We always had a cow or two show up around the ranch with their long legged, wobbly, red calves. We would get used to seeing some often enough to identify each one.

One Sunday morning I was on my way to church at Glennallen and I had to walk up the muddy road to where the car was parked. When I arrived at the car and was changing my

muddy shoes, I kept hearing a groaning noise I couldn't identify. It sounded like a wounded animal back in the brush. I
planned to send Bud to investigate as soon as I got back. When
I returned, there in the road close to where I would have to
park the car again, was a cow moose and her new born calf. I
had never realized that a wild animal mother suffered, or at
least sounded like she did, when giving birth.

We acquired a grazing lease from the BLM in the Snag River
drainage near Wolf Lake and started taking the horses over there
about mid June. They were turned loose and regathered a few
days before the hunting season started. We had lucked out and
bought another horse from an outfitter who was so tired of re-

LeNora on Tony.

catching that horse that he wanted it out of his outfit. This horse
was slipping away at the most inconvenient times, heading back
home leaving the hunter to walk. Well I fell in love with that
pretty palomino and claimed him for my own. I named him
Tony and we got along just great. It didn't take me long to
figure out what his thinking was. He pretended to be innocent.
He was content to just take me long to catch on to his sly plans.
He would stand, pretending to be half asleep, but the minute a

person dropped the reins or a stake rope, he would walk away and walk too fast to be caught unless you went after him on another horse. He only pulled that on me one time. He stayed just out of my reach when he had jerked the rope loose out of my hand. I was walking him around the lake to stake him with the other horses. If I ran he trotted faster. I think he enjoyed this as a game. I would have to walk a few miles back to camp that day had not one of the boys seen what happened and caught Tony before he reached the corral back at Wolf Lake. He was always the first horse waiting at the corral for oats.

I didn't like to let anyone else ride my horse, but some times it was necessary, but he made a good dude horse. This rider was alerted to Tony's cute tricks but there was still a couple of times at Wolf lake when one of the wranglers had to ride clear back to base camp and lead him back.

After we started getting repeat clients for the fall hunts at Wolf Lake, we hired a couple for the season. He was an assistant guide and she cooked in base camp. That left me free to cook for the clients and crew at the Cotton Wood Camp. This spike camp was a five hour ride with the pack train following the trail Bud had blazed at the base of steep hills traversing the canyon where Cotton Creek water sings rushing down from the rocky hills and spreads out over a wide bar past the tent camp we set up. I considered this cooking job the best time of the hunting seasons. I made up the groceries for a crew of six men and myself, to last five or six days, then pack it all in the wooden panniers to be packed so the boxes would weigh about the same and balanced when a pack horse was carrying it. After one experience when a pack horse got scared, shucked its pack scattering groceries in all directions as well as the broken glass and mantle for the Coleman lanterns, I became an expert at this packing job. Regardless of how it arrived it got to its destination in usable shape. My next task was riding Tony at the tail end of the pack string to keep an eye on the packs on the horses ahead of me in case a pack starts shifting.

Happy in my new task and on that first ride to this camp, I was laughing about that first woman we hired as a cook. She was the wife of an outfitter we knew and we felt lucky to have her in our camp for the hunting season. When I asked her why we were so lucky she said we paid her good wages but when she cooked for her husband's hunting camps she usually would be taken for granted and not only didn't get paid for her efforts but without even as much as a thank you. I thought; oh well——welcome to the group: 'Wives not receiving their dues.'

We had a comfortable tent camp set up in the trees close to the creek at Cottonwood Camp. Before we started taking clients here to hunt, Bud had hauled a variety of camp gear in here on a winter trail using the weasel. He built a high cache and we left empty fifty-five-gallon drums with bear proof rims, now we could store everything we didn't carry back when we broke camp. After an early breakfast the men all left camp for the day.

LeNora, the cook, at Cottonwood Camp.

They had their lunches so the day was my own until dinner time. I'd carry my rifle and a berry bucket and spend most of a lovely after noon in a blueberry patch on a hillside, always in open country where I was in no danger of suddenly or unexpectedly meeting a grizzly. There were plenty of them around according to tracks on the creek bar. I would not have been too popular in camp had I shot a bear when we had hunters who had paid big money to come shoot a grizzly bear. However, no one complained about the blueberry pie or pancakes served at the table.

One time when we were at Cottonwood Creek camp a bear stampeded the horses out of camp. While Bud and his assistant guide walked back to Wolf Lake to bring them back, I climbed the mountain behind our camp with a very pleasant client waiting to make his next hunt. He had collected his trophy Dall ram two days earlier but wanted pictures of the ewes and lambs we could see from camp. He invited me to go with him and I didn't hesitate. Something as unexpected and enjoyable as climbing those beautiful hills on a sunny fall day was a real bonus in trade for those meals I cooked in camp.

I don't remember that we ever had a client who complained about anything in this camp. They always got the game they came to hunt and they especially like the country here and at Wolf Lake. Most times there would be two or three men who came on these hunts. It never fails that something interesting happened that was etched into your memory, or about the hunter. I remember a party of three men who all came from the same city back east. Two of them had always previously hunted together but it was the first time this friend was invited to hunt with them. They played tricks on him and teased him about anything they could think up. He took it all good naturedly. One afternoon all three returned from their hunt early and offered to go pick blueberries for a pie since I hadn't had any leisure time that day. The two jokesters returned long before their friend with there buckets seemingly full. About an hour later the friend showed up with a full bucket. When I took the few berries off the top of buckets using moss as a filling, there wasn't enough between the two buckets for a pie, the third man's full bucket was. When I was cleaning the berries to make the pie this man slipped into the kitchen without them seeing him and asked if I'd be willing to help him turn the tables on his friends. I was happy to oblige. He didn't participate in the laughter but he had the last laugh when those two men looked at two small blueberry pies, no bigger than three inches across, setting in front of them and their friend had a normal size pie that he shared with the crew, but not with them. Those men were fun to have in a hunting camp and kept everyone laughing at the never ending jokes. They were serious hunters as well and the kind all guides like for a hunt.

Rudolf was one of our saddle horses with a personality that

didn't qualify him for a dude horse. Most hunters who book a hunt with an outfitter who uses horses are used to riding. A horse knows this and can sense when there is fear. They take advantage of this and will go off the trail to go under a branch to brush off a rider. Rudolf had a tough mouth and would hold the bit in his teeth and wander off the trail if he thought there was something to eat there and almost pull the reins out of the rider's hand. We had a hunter who didn't like to ride a horse and that was why Rudolf was in camp this day and it was up to me to move him and the other horse left in camp, to another grazing area. I had left them close to camp while I was busy. Late that afternoon I rode the first one around the lake to the opposite side from camp. I walked back to relocate Rudolf and decided I would lead him instead of riding. He was so eager to get over there with the other horse he took a short cut straight across the lake!!! I was pulling and cussing him, using some of Bud's type of authority language, but it was ignored. He had me at a disadvantage and knew it. I emerged from the lake soaking wet and thinking up more names to let him know how unhappy I was with him and didn't see the men returning early from their hunt. They had come out from a trail in the woods not far from where I was tying that horse to a stake. They were laughing and let me know they had heard the names I was calling that smart-ass horse. They knew I was mad and said I was doing a very professional job of word painting. I was the brunt of a lot of jokes the rest of that day. Those hunters didn't know my use of words were that colorful.

Another time I was riding Tony at the end of the pack train when we were returning to Wolf Lake after the hunt was over at Cotton Wood Camp. I was watching a dude riding the horse Baldy, with a pack horse in between. Baldy preferred to jump a small stream, or a fallen log in preference to stepping over it. I had a glimpse of one of the pack horses going around a bend before it went out of my sight. I thought the rider had seen the log but Baldy jumped across it and the rider was picking himself up off the trail when I caught up to him. He was embarrassed but not hurt. He said he guessed he dozed of. I was watching ahead and let Tony choose the trail and he didn't go around a soft spot by a fallen tree and as he crossed his hind quarters slipped into a hole that a fallen tree had left. I stepped out of the saddle and released the belly strap and slipped the saddle off. Then talking to him and pulling on the reins he managed to get his hind feet out of the hole and onto solid ground. The man ahead of me wanted to catch up with the rest of the outfit and have Bud, or one of the boys return to help me. "Bud knows I can handle it," I assured him while putting the saddle back on and thanked him for his offer to help. Tony was excited enough without some one trying to help who didn't understand horses. I was pleased with myself that I took care of the situation without calling for help but that man just couldn't believe that Bud didn't come back, to see what was holding us up so long.

We caught up with the others waiting, Bud's comment was I should have seen it was obvious that eight horses ahead of us had gone around that hole yet Tony didn't ! "Okay Tony, we should be so talented. You heard what the boss man said! Don't let it happen again!" I said while petting and loving his pretty tan hide. "When we get back to the corral I'll give you an extra hand full of oats."

Chapter Eight

Grizzly Bears at Eagle Trail Ranch

When the horses were returned to the ranch at the end of the hunting season at Wolf Lake they were taken to the Copper River and turned loose until the snow was too deep for them to forage. Bud flew over them often keeping track on how they were faring. They always stayed together and were ready to come home where the oats and hay was easier to get. When the ice on the river was strong enough for a horse to cross, Bud would take a bucket and shovel, dig up sand to make a gritty path on the slippery glare ice, then lead one horse at a time across it to the bar on the home trail. I always went along to help but not one single horse would cross the ice if I was leading it. They trusted Bud but not me. They must have thought if they slipped and fell I wouldn't be able to help them back on their feet. They would not walk out on slick ice without Bud. It was comical to watch Bud leading a horse as it would hold its head over Buds shoulder leaning on him for support. He talked soothingly to the horse all the way across, often it was only a short distance. I asked him why he didn't sing to it and he said the horses preferred listening to him talking and if he started singing he was sure they would all run in the opposite direction. I readily agreed. My singing wasn't any better.

I think I was too interested in what was in the mail and forgot to sing while walking on the road where the brush and willows crowded close. When I sing loudly that is enough to scare anything away within a mile or so. I have heard that playing dead might be the right thing to do if a bear is chomping on you, but running from one is never recommended unless there's a tree close to climb. I know from experience one can move fast under certain conditions.

I became accustomed to the bears at Tanada Lake. Although I think they were the ones that really adjusted to us and didn't bother us much except the one that broke into the lodge. Maybe he told the others that the man who lived there got paid for people to come and shoot bears. At Eagle Trail Ranch, there were more bears around, either that or they just came closer.

Cleaning up after bear damage.

Frequently we would find muddy paw prints on a window where one had looked in but hadn't tried to get inside. This would happen usually when we were away. Yet there was that vandal who tore up the airplane. Another time one made so much noise trying to get moose meat out of the station wagon that it woke us up, when Bud opened the window on the side close to it, the bear growled and made a rush like it would come right in. Bud slammed the window, picked up the rifle he always kept handy, went out the back door and started shooting in the air and yelling for it to get going or it was going to look different without its fur coat. That bear believed him because it wasn't around at daylight. We had been too tired to take care of the meat when we got home late that night. Our mistake! Our station wagon had teeth and claw scratches as reminders of that bear's visit. After we had a garage built and a Witte generator chugging loudly inside it, we'd find grizzly tracks coming or going, on the horse trail from the Copper River. We also discovered they would bypass the garage and house, then using our access road they would go to and cross the highway

I came close to meeting a grizzly bear on our road one summer morning when I had walked up to our mail box and half way back a beautifully furred, chocolate brown grizzly came out of the bushes on one side and crossed the road not fifteen feet ahead of me. If I had been walking faster we would have met face to face. That bear didn't even turn his head to look at me. It was on its way like it knew where it was going and no big hurry to get there. It disappeared in the willows on the opposite side. Me? I slowly backed up and kept backing up expecting it to come back and take a look to see what that was in the road so close by. I was so impressed by what a huge bear it was that all the while I was backing up I was admiring it. Its long, rich brown fur rippling in the breeze that was blowing toward me.

After a grizzly visit.

Had the breeze been blowing from the other direction I'm sure he would have looked in my direction. I was glad I had taken my shower, or maybe he just couldn't smell well. Where ever that bear went it never showed up around our place, seems I was the only one so privileged to see it that close and with no bad memory of our meeting. There were no trees close enough to climb if my intentions were to climb one.

When my experienced guide-husband was teaching me the ways of the wild animals, he stressed what to do in bear country. Stay alert and watching; read their intentions. (Oh yeah,—sounds good on paper, but how long could I stand watching a grizzly long enough to read its intentions?) One learns the art of moving gently, without suddenness, was the first lesson. Always remember this is their country and we are the trespassers. The key is not to be a threat to them or startle one unexpectedly.

No bear was going to keep me out of a berry patch when the blueberries were ripe and pick a patch with a super abundance near the road in open areas, but if a bear showed up it was all his. I'd get in my parked car and find another patch.

Not long after we moved to Eagle Trail Ranch I was bent over on a logging trail to examine some fresh tracks close to the cabin. I don't know what alerted me to look down the trail behind me in time to see a grizzly bear come in sight around a bend running full bore in my direction. I only made three jumps to the cabin door before I looked back. Later I discovered the bear was after a little calf moose that, along with its mother, had ran down the trail ahead of the bear and had jumped a berm close to where I had seen the tracks. I hadn't waited to find out if that bear might have mistaken me for the calf as I was on the trail wearing my tan hide jacket.

Bud was usually home from the spring bear hunts on the Alaska Peninsula by the time the bears were out of hibernation, I was also gone for the hunting season at Wolf Lake so didn't always have to deal with a bear problem. That was Bud's department to deal with. I was called on when there were horses that needed attention, or if Bud or Colin were not home.

We had one horse that was wise enough to jump the fence, lift the latch then let the other horses out. It seems they knew that June was the season and they wanted to be hard to find when it was that time of the year to take them to Wolf Lake. I would fly with Bud to locate them and we'd find them standing in thick timber quite a distance to have to go after them. If Bud was walking into the area the one with a bell on would stand still (not letting the bell jangle.) I never referred to our horses as dumb animals.

There was the day I felt like I was a dumb female for letting myself be talked into hauling two of our heaviest horses in the horse trailer from the ranch to the border. At the time we still had the second hand Ford pickup and it didn't have the engine power needed to pull two of the steep hills, if you didn't have the momentum to keep moving. (Not enough HP to pull the hills—hence the term horse power.) I was thinking I'd be in big trouble if a slow motor home or loaded truck ahead of me slowed me down. Bud could have handled it with no effort, but I couldn't believe he had that much confidence in my ability to safely deliver his precious horses or perhaps it was because there was no one else to do it. The person who was scheduled to haul those horses with his own pickup wasn't able to come the day we were going to leave. I am sure I could have driven that two ton truck of ours but I was smart enough not to drive it because I might be called on to haul six horses so Bud could be free to fly the airplane home. I was under the impression I had enough work to do.

The first two years that we took the horses in to Wolf Lake the Chisana River was high and some places was too deep and the wranglers had to pick the best place to swim them across. The second year I rode in with them to the river and took movies of the horses swimming across. Bud would cross with a five man raft holding the rope tied to a horse's halter, lead a swimming horse across, tie it up and cross back for another one until all were across. When they were swimming they held their head high out of the water, lips up as far as they would go exposing their big teeth, looking ridiculous. We walked three miles back to the highway, after seeing the boys on their way to Wolf Lake. Bud and I drove back to the ranch and he'd get in the plane and fly over to check on them. Then when the horses were turned loose for the summer on the grazing lease we had there, he would fly the boys out to the highway and they would drive our truck back to the ranch and be back to work for us again for the hunting season.

Bud started flying over to the Chisana later in June, watching and waiting, until the river was low enough before he would get the horses on their way to Wolf Lake. He learned it was better to wait until timing and water level was right. He was always too impatient to get things done and on to the next job waiting. That was when I discovered he didn't know everything after all (I hadn't forgotten the time we were whipsawing lumber those early years at Tanada Lake and after a few long, hard days, discovered a dry log cut so much easier than a green one.) However, I trusted his judgement at all times regardless.

It was at the same crossing where we took our horses across the Chisana that a well known bush pilot, Bud Hickathier, drowned while swimming his horses across. His outfitting head-quarters was at Chisana. He was riding a young horse and no one was ever sure how the accident happened as his body was never found. He was a friend who stopped often at the ranch whenever he was in the area.

It was the fourth year we had our horses, that a mare we bought was already bred and was due to drop her colt in the spring. She had an adorable gold foal, and I named her Goldie. She was mine right from the first day I saw her and as she grew I spent every minute I could leading her around with her pretty halter on and teaching her tricks. She was too young that year to take along with the horses so we boarded her and her mother at a friends ranch until we were back from the fall hunts.

Goldie was six months old when we were home again from hunts at Wolf Lake. An early snow and sleet storm hit before Bud had time to go bring the mare and colt home. He had tried once but the hills were too icy for the pickup pulling the horse trailer so he returned and said he would get them as soon as the hills were sanded. He knew I was looking forward to seeing my colt again. The day he did go to get them, I couldn't go with him. Instead Bob Nelson went and they had plans to cut wood logs for weight for the pickup, doing the logging near a old road off the highway. I was in the kitchen when I saw the pickup back up to unload the logs. The two of them stayed out there so after unloading, I started out the door to investigate, as Bud came in Bob headed out into the woods. It looked as though he was in a hurry to get behind a tree?

"How did the trip go, I can hardly wait to get supper over so I can go see her and her mama," I said. "I'll bet she has grown a lot."

Bob came back in before Bud answered and looked at me then to Bud and asked him if he told me. Bud shook his head and looked at a loss for words. Bob intervened and said; "The colt had died three days before they got there!" Those people had found her stretched out dead with the mare standing close by. They said she hadn't shown any signs of being sick, as many years as they had horses and raised colts, they didn't have the slightest clue as to why she died. People who know horses know this happens at times and unless you have a veterinarian come and diagnose the reason it died, one has to accept it.

Bob looked at me and said; "it's bad enough that Bud hated

to tell you the colt died and if that wasn't bad enough when he backed up to unload the wood he backed over your Siamese kitten! Neither one of us saw it when he was backing up. We didn't want you to see it so I buried it back in the woods."

I have always had a cat and managed to keep one from the time it was a kitten until a hawk or animal made a meal of it. They get wise, and are alert to the dangers they face when they roam in the woods. A few I have had over the years lived several years. One I had was twenty three years old when he died of old age. He roamed at will all the years at Eagle Trail Ranch and had to be a wise cat to avoid all the animals that he came in contact with. He even raced foxes around the yard without getting caught by them. I had a cat that always went out to the horses with me and rode on the back of the fattest pack horse. He learned early to keep out from under their feet and which horse objected to a cat on its back.

I hadn't let this kitten out doors unless I was with her so she wasn't wise to big wheels backing up. I had let her out so she could greet them on arrival and get the expected petting she was used to from both of them. In my book - WIND ON THE WATER - I wrote about the cat I took with me to Tanada Lake when we had our huskies. How she survived five sled dogs plus riding on the sled they had to pull. Huskies are not known to have a love or tolerance for cats.

The last year Colin went to school in Valdez we drove and planned to stay a few days, then bring him home for the Christmas holidays. I took Mama-Kitty and her three six weeks old kittens with us. The temperature was down to forty degrees below zero on our return. The road was blown shut with hard drifts and we had to park the car a short distance off the highway and walk in to the cabin. I carried the three kittens in my parka. Mama - Kitty didn't want to be carried but she ran along side or behind me and frequently asked to see her babies. She wanted to be sure I had them. She would often ride draped across Bud's shoulders around the ranch but now she didn't want to share the space on his back with the pack he was carrying. She didn't want Colin to carry her because he was carrying the little black puppy some one in Valdez had given him.

It takes a long time to warm a cabin that has been left unheated for twenty four hours or more. Bud was faithful to leave a generous supply of wood and the type of kindling he whittled into slivers attached to a dry stick so it started a fire in the heater or kitchen stoves fast. After a long, late drive home and a long walk, we would all be too tired to wait for the rooms to warm up so we each stood close to the heater holding a pillow and a blanket until warm then into a cold bed.

The next day or later (when time permitted,) Bud plowed the road open and we had our mode of transportation setting by the cabin again. Mail days it generally took Bud two hours to get the station wagon warmed and ready to go for the mail. The battery was in the house behind the heater stove (put there after it was used last.) The barrel stove is big enough for all the gear that laps around it, cans of oil for the car, a container for the drained oil for the airplane, heavy gloves, mukluks, shoe-pac, flying pants and parka. Now he sets the blow torch under the engine to heat the oil pan and keeps an eye on it in case it catches on fire. Meanwhile he is shoveling out the snow drifts in front of the car, plus the steep driveway where the wind made drifts after he had plowed it.

When I hear the car running I put on my winter boots, parka and gloves, make sure I have the grocery list and mail to go. If the wind has been blowing a gale for more than a few days then I am ready to get out of this place for awhile. When we get one of those winds that last for days, howling weirdly around the cabin, it eventually gets on one's nerves. Even if we are not sure mail has arrived at the Slana post office, we have to go see.

This is a typical drive out to the highway on our road after it has been snowing and the wind drifting snow across the road. Bud is so sure he can make it out through the drifts with out having to plow snow again, he says he has two shovels in the car in case—!

Pouring on the gas and bouncing over, or through the crusted snow, we sway into a deep rut under the snow that nearly throws the car off into the snow bank on the opposite side. Bud jerks it back into the road and it slides into the snow bank on this other side. We both get out and shovel the car out for the third time before reaching the highway. While Bud is shoveling through the berm the snowplow had pushed up in our drive-way (when clearing the highway,) he is wasting breath cursing the grader operator. I stand out on the cleared highway ready

to motion him to barrel out over the balance of the snow berm
when there is no traffic coming. He has to back up then make
a run to get up the uphill grade and out onto the icy pavement.
A good thing that station wagon is a sturdy built vehicle and
can take that punishment, I would remind him.

Mail is due at the Slana post office once a week, but seldom
arrives on schedule due to road and, weather conditions. Not
long ago it only came once a month unless some one went to
Gakona then they brought everyone's mail. Maybe the mail
would be there, or maybe not. Heading back home Bud would
yell "hang on" as he gunned the motor and put it in low gear. I
was already hanging on as the Chrysler careened back and forth
through the drifts. My feet were braced against the floor boards.
If lucky we'll make it all the way back to the cabin. If not we'll
walk home and dig it out the next day.

Once I was determined I was going regardless of hubby's
advice to wait and he would go with me. Backing up on a steep
hill to get a run at it, I backed up into the deepest snow on the
road. Bud was all morning digging the station wagon out. To
keep peace between us for the day I ignored his tirade about
women drivers don't seem to have the touch. Gee, I'm thinking.
Don't I get any credit for all those years I have been driving and
taking care of all the situations I get faced with. "Had you not
been home I would have eventually dug it out. I wanted to go
today so I thank you for your help," I said as I took the wheel
after he drove the station wagon to the top of the icy hill.

The pleasant surprise this strenuous winter day was mail had
arrived and everybody for miles around was there. We had long
overdue magazines and letters. No one speaks until their mail is
eagerly scanned for the latest news. Then people are standing
around in groups visiting. I doubt if the service men in the Armed
Forces overseas looked forward to mail any more than we do.
This was a bonus for my effort in getting there.

I think it was the second Christmas we lived at the ranch that
the highways were all blown shut with blizzard wind, snow slides
and drifts. The last mail day there hadn't been a thing in the mail
sacks but five newspapers apiece for the ten families. As soon as
flying weather permitted we flew to Gakona where there was a
landing strip and that was as far as the mail had gotten. We had a
load of mail to take back, ours as well as many others. There was

a New Years party scheduled at the Gakona lodge the next night so it was a good excuse to stay overnight with our friends. I don't think anyone in the community, or anywhere within miles, stayed home that night, even though it was forty below zero. Everybody danced and sang, indulged freely of liquid refreshments. It was one of those spontaneous fun parties. Everyone had fun and were feeling no pain when the New Year arrived. The next morning there weren't any of the pilots out early fire-potting their aircraft.

I never ceased to admire the things Bud Conkle accomplished. Once he made up his mind to do something he figured out how and when he was going to do it. I went with him when he unloaded the weasel from the truck at the highway and drove it sixty miles to Wolf Lake. He was back from the polar bear hunts early in April, the weather was moderate and it sounded like an interesting two or three day trip. It ended up a five day trip plowing through deep snow camping every night. My job was to go ahead on snowshoes, when it was close to time to spend the night, then shovel out a clearing for the tent. Shoveling out five feet of snow took me long enough so he arrived about the time I had it cleared. The brilliant moonlight nights made up for each long hard days work clearing snow that stuck in the weasel tracks and that also made for a memorable trip. A pilot friend flew us home from Wolf Lake. The following August after we had taken the weasel over to Wolf Lake I made another memorable trip in it. My brother, his wife and my sister, arrived from California to visit at the ranch and be there for my birthday—August 10. Also that is opening day of sheep season. We didn't have any nonresident hunters booked until the following week. Bud talked my brother into obtaining a non- resident hunting license and try for a Dall sheep from our hunting camp at Wolf Lake. He said us gals just as well go too and we'd have a party over there. Sounded good and he flew us all from the highway to Wolf Lake. He had a spike camp up a canyon from the lake with a tent frame and cache, he wanted to leave camp gear and canned things for the next hunt. Good planning I'd say. The two men climbed high in the sheep hills while the three of us climbed a lower hill to enjoy the scenery, the lovely sunny day and pick the luscious blue berries from the hillside thick with their bushes.

It started sprinkling lightly with ominous clouds moving across the high peaks. We hurried back to the camp, got a fire going, but had to wait for the men to come set up the tent. We all had our sleeping bags for an overnight stay if need be. The two men returned late afternoon in a down pour making it difficult coming back down the steep inclines with heavy packs. Brother Harold had a nice ram. To make a sheep hunt in Alaska had been a long time dream for him. Those clouds were serious and the rain was pouring down on us. Bud said we have to get back across the creek or the way this rain is coming down we won't be able to get across without swimming. That was an unpleasant thought. It had been such a nice trip going up the narrow canyon between the snow capped peaks. Why did it have to rain now? When we arrived at the creek there was a five foot bank we'd have to go down.

"Oh-oh. Are these city folks rugged enough to walk all the way back to the lake?

A grizzly was determined to get into the garage.

It's doubtful. So what shall we do?" I asked Bud, as he was studying the situation.

"It will be worse by tomorrow and we'll still have to walk back to the lake," was his answer.

His solution to that problem was putting us all to work carrying rocks, the bigger the better, piling them at the base of the bank for a ramp to drive the weasel down. He carried the biggest ones he could find. If we sweated doing all that manual labor for the length of time it took, we couldn't tell the difference between rain drops or sweat. It was still a steep incline when Bud said he would try driving down into the creek that was spread across the bar but not to deep. He said best he try it alone.

No one insisted on riding down with him. We held our breath expecting the weasel to roll over forward or sideways over that most unprofessional ramp. It rocked and screeched but with Bud's skilled handling, it went down safe with no break in the sensitive tracks that rocks can easily damage.

Back at Wolf Lake very late in the night, tired and hungry, Bud told them he wasn't real sure we'd be riding back in the weasel or on our own two feet. It did give them a good story to tell about their Alaska experience. He said he could hear their unvoiced thoughts when thinking about walking back in the dark over rocks and foot tangling brush, wondering why they had let themselves in for that adventure. We cut the birthday cake and toasted to another birthday for me, then Bud flew us (one at a time) out to the highway. We overnighted at the ranch then I drove them back to Anchorage where they were to catch a midnight flight home. At a birthday dinner in a popular restaurant before they left, they reminded me that if I expect a birthday party I had best move my birthday to a different date than opening day of Dall sheep season in the Wrangell Mountains!

Driving to Anchorage had left me with no time for personal shopping. It was time to load the station wagon with case groceries and fresh produce, but leaving room for the luggage of the client I was to meet on his arrival at the airport, then drive him back to Grace Lake on the highway near the border where Bud would be meeting us.

Often my friend Daphne McMahan would be loading their station wagon at Prairie Market for their hunts while I was there and that was visiting time squeezed in to exchange news since last time we were together, maybe it hadn't been since in the spring or summer. It was a pleasure to meet some of the other pilot-guide's wives who were on the same mission. We were rushed for time but, for us it was like kids with candy, we took time for a "quickie" visit that often shortened our time at the next place or just made us plain late.

Chapter Nine

Another Pilot in the Family

How fast the years go by, and now my young son is a grown man, and he also is a pilot. It wasn't very long ago he sat on my lap, and his daddy was the pilot. Now he is the pilot in the cockpit and I sit in the seat behind him, remembering many flights in past years when three of us flew places. Colin had a private pilot's license when he was sixteen. When he returned home after a three year enlistment in the U.S. Army—overseas duty in Germany—he received his commercial license. He then did most of the flying for our Eagle Trail Ranch big game hunting business. He was a natural at the controls of the Super Cub. I jumped at the chance to fly with him whenever possible. His dad would hint Colin was a better pilot than he was, but didn't want to admit it. Now Bud had an aerial wolf hunting partner and I had two pilots to worry about when they were overdue.

The first flight I took with Colin, after his return from the military, was a flight from Cobb lake at Eagle Trail Ranch, to Tanada Lake. It was a 'memory lane' time for both of us to talk about those past years where he had spent his early years, and for us to see the changes the new owners had made. Tanada Lake Lodge was now a modern wilderness lodge, showers in the guest cabins, refrigerator, electricity, and a gas cook stove in the kitchen. A generator and water system made quite the difference from when I was the cook in that lodge.

There was no guests at the lodge the day in June when we landed there. The flying weather was perfect for a swing around into the mountains before we landed, then a short visit, and tour of the improvements by the care taker. Colin had to go climb one of his favorite hills while the day was still young. While he was enjoying his special pastime, I was walking the shore line of Tanada Lake around the point, out of sight of the lodge, pretending I was still living here and treasuring the time from kitchen duties, while watching the sand pipers softly piping along the shore, their long pointed beaks needling the sand. Farther out brilliantly colored mallards were sending gentle wakes as they swam arrogantly past a family of dung colored mud hens. High in the blue sky a bald eagle mounted a vortex of air, wheeled smartly, its wings spread for a long glide. Its eye was on one of the young ducks swimming with its family, but I raised my arms as it flew close and it sailed away in the distance to hunt some place else for an after noon snack. I was in hopes I hadn't ruined that big bird's day when I was having such an enjoyable day myself, and watching the ducks enjoying theirs. I was thinking all those feathered birds I was watching could be, most likely were descendants of the ones I used to watch swimming, raising their young and then leave when winter was soon due. It would seem strange to me that for another few years to come I was only a guest at Tanada Lake Lodge. It belongs to somebody else now, and another change in my life I have accepted.

It was on Mother's Day two years later that Colin asked me if I'd like to fly with him up to Mt. Sanford, my reply was; yes. His goal was what looked like a smoking crater that was creating a lot of excitement in the immediate area. From our house we could look right at the eternally snow covered mountain. A few of the local pilots flew up to take a look, but when some geologists flew up to also take a look, they discovered a deep slide and the snow that fell into the crater was creating steam, not smoke.

I have always liked to go flying with Colin, and within minutes I had my flying suit on, and settled into the passenger seat of our Super Cub. From the plane's side window I watched the snow covered tundra, flying over the Nabesna glacier to look for the Cessna 180 that two men had left sitting there after an emergency landing the day before, Colin wanted to see if it was still there. We didn't find it, but then we didn't spend much time looking ether. Then to gain the altitude needed to fly up near the top of 14,500 foot Mt. Sanford, my pilot circled in wide circles and then more circles, the higher we flew, the smaller and narrower the Cub felt to me, and it looked a long ways from the ground. At 13,000 feet, flying over huge pointed boulders protruding out of the snow, I am thinking this would be a poor place for an emergency landing. There just wasn't any space between those boulders for anything but a helicopter. At 14,000 feet we started smelling the fumes coming from Mt. Wrangell which always emits fumes. Then I started smelling smoke, and I was sure it was coming from the airplane engine. I was watching the instrument panel over Colin's shoulder, and looking for a reaction from him. Soon he turned to ask me if I smelled smoke.

"Yes, I sure do. Can you tell if it's a fire in the engine? Are you going to make an emergency landing, or can you glide back to the Nabesna glacier?" I was throwing questions at him without waiting for an answer. He turned to tell me he thought it was an oil drip on the manifold pipe, and nothing serious.

Then he said; " Oh, now I know what caused the smoke. I turned the radio on to see if I could contact the radio station at Gulkana and it was dust or fuzz had created the sparks and smoke, when I turned the radio off the smoke is gone," he explained to my relief. He knew it was okay but I wasn't so sure.

I was looking below us at the jagged rocks and wind-pulsed snow wondering what the airplane and we would look like had we crashed there and no radio to call for help. Morbid thought. I was expecting him to head back down toward the glacier, knowing that with the long wing span of the Cub it could glide on for a landing on the glacier if need be. Like father, like son, he said he would make a wide turn and fly close to the slide area so we could get pictures. I had forgotten all about pictures and why we had flown up there. I am thinking about this later and telling myself that this was once I was there to know why we were delayed, Bud would have been home worrying why we hadn't returned if we'd had an emergency landing. This would have given him an insight into my problems when left home worrying. It would have been an uneventful flight back to the ranch if it hadn't been for the two unusually big gray timber wolves we flew over that were gorging on a moose kill. Colin had spotted their tracks and the bird activity in the area and as the plane neared what looked like a fresh kill, those two wolves lost interest in the dead moose and headed flat out for the safety of timber. Colin flew low over them as they were in a hurry to outdistance the big bird flying in their direction. It was a thrilling sight to watch their long, loping glide, stretched out and running. They were identical size and color phase.

Flying over vast acres of wilderness Alaska one often sees sights one wouldn't be in a position to see or watch other wise. I was flying with Bud one fall and we flew over five big grizzly bears all fishing in a shallow bay of the Copper River. All those grizzlies were the same size and identical in color. What was unusual was the color phase of a golden tan with a lighter tan wide band around their necks. Most likely it was a sow with two cubs and the other with one cub. The sows could have been sisters.

I sometimes flew with Bud to make an air drop at one of our spike camps during the fall hunts. There were times the client and their guide would be in an isolated camp longer than planned and still staying to collect the game they were hunting. If they needed more groceries dropped to them they had a signal to let the pilot know when he flew over to check on them. Groceries are packed in a special way, so they will survive the drop from the airplane, without breakage or smashed if it lands on sharp rocks, or in water, in the event the aim is not calculated just right. I was proud of my aim when a box of needed groceries landed close to the camp tent. It was always up to me to package these air drops. Cans that would crush were padded and nothing crowded, allowing room for a jarring stop. With long streamers attached in the event the package landed in the trees of some place hard to find. Bud often had to do this alone and one time his aim was too good. The heavy box landed right through the side of the tent tearing a long ragged slit above the table. Whoever was to make the drop from the airplane was instructed about the exact time to push the box out when the pilot raises his arm, be sure to send it far enough out past the pontoons so it doesn't hit them and be sure the streamers are wrapped in the right way so they unfurl properly or they will tangle on the struts or tail feathers.

One early summer Bud flew a miner out in the bush some isolated place, and there was no place for an airplane to land. The 'Old Boy' directed Bud to where his cabin was and he would drop his supplies, then walk in from the river near by. Bud had instructed him about the timing, but the minute Bud lifted the side window in preparation for the drop, the man started tossing boxes out, and Bud never did see his cabin, he could only hope the man found them all because the boxes were scattered amidst thick trees and hundreds of feet apart.

There have been stories written about a few of those early Bush-Pilots who made airdrops to isolated mines, and it didn't always land where intended. A story told about a noted pilot who made a direct hit that went through the improvised roof of the outhouse, and into the muck below. It happened to be the steaks for the working crew. The story told on that pilot lasted for many years, told and retold.

One late August I flew with Bud from the highway, at Grace Lake, near the border, to Wolf Lake. The hunters, the cook and crew were already in camp, and Bud had made a trip with all the groceries for the fall hunts and returned for me. I was the last one to be flown in. A snow storm was brewing, and he rushed me to hurry and get the house trailer closed, and the station wagon parked, so we could be ahead of the storm. I had just returned from picking up our two clients at Gulkana, and after taking them to the lake where he flew them over to wolf lake, where he left the plane parked, and walked about a quarter of a mile to meet me. It must have been in that short time that a hitchhiker on the road saw Bud leave, and took all the emergency rations out of the Cub. We were too busy, and in a hurry, and didn't miss them then. We flew across the flat area and nearing the mountains the snow came down so heavy it was too dangerous to keep going ahead, and snowing too heavy to turn back. Bud made the decision to set down on a lake he was familiar with, and wait out the storm. It lasted three days. We had our sleeping bags but no emergency rations or tent. Bud had his waterproof match case and pocket knife with him, a hatchet and his pistol was tucked in behind the forward seat. Lucky for us those two handy items were overlooked by the thief. There was plenty of dry wood around the lake, and we kept a warm fire going all the time, it kept us busy just gathering wood. We ate ducks for breakfast, dinner and snacks for lunch. Bud amused himself sneaking up close to where the ducks had also taken refuge. If he didn't get one with a first pistol shot, they all flew away into the snow covered sky or settled across the lake with heavy snow to cover their sanctuary. We then had to wait for another unwary group to land close to shore.

Everyone at Wolf Lake would assume we were held up at our trailer near the border at Scotty Creek and the people running the lodge at Scotty Creek, Glen and Ethel Stoneman, would assume we had made it to Wolf Lake. Had we crashed, and been too badly injured to walk back, no one would be looking for us. After three days of sleeping under the protective branches of a snow laden spruce tree, we were ready to move. The snow had almost stopped, but now a heavy fog set in. It was slowly lifting and Bud had the engine of the plane warmed up, and ready to fly (as soon as he could see across the lake.) He was familiar with the route across the flat tundra, but nearing the mountains the fog was still too low to clear the low hills and he was heading for the pass where Wolf Lake nestled at the base. Believe me, I was praying and watching my pilot sweating, as he was intently watching for familiar land marks across the tundra, with nothing but sameness, and knowing he was getting closer, and closer, to the steep hills. Tall trees would have spanked the undersides of the Super Cub, had there been any in that pass at the end of Wolf Lake. In camp they heard the familiar sound of the airplane approaching and every lantern in camp was lit and set out at the opposite end of the lake to guide the plane. It was turning dark and the water was calm with a black shadow of the mountain across it. Caught in situations like this, some times the pilot will call it "the-moment-of-truth." Will it be an uneventful landing or a crash! I had a feeling my pilot was as happy as I was to see the lights allowing him to make direct approach and a normal landing, then taxi to the tiedown spot where onlookers gathered. They were generous in their compliments about his low flying ability and the smooth landing the minute he exited the plane. He shrugged his shoulders giving the impression it was "just a piece of cake."

In order to use as much of the small lake as possible, for just this type of pancake landing, Bud had previously cut a swath of the trees the width of the Super Cub wing span, over the low hill at one end allowing the plane to skim the hill top, then drop in short onto the lake, giving the pilot more lake ahead to taxi and make the turn to where the passenger and contents of the plane were to be unloaded. One not familiar with a bush pilot's techniques of accomplishing his goals, often made interesting remarks when their feet were on solid ground. Both pilot's, Bud and Colin, had this approach to Wolf Lake down to perfection from their many landings even with a cross wind. Their takeoffs were at the opposite end with no bank and no trees.

Colin was the pilot on a windy day when he was flying some of the clients out to the highway. When their hunts were over he'd fly the next hunters in to camp. The turbulence was rough and bouncing the loaded Cub up and down. It didn't encourage Joe (I have long since forgotten his last name—but not the remark he made) to do any more flying in a small airplane. Later he was telling his guide that he planned to ride out to the highway with the boys when they took the horses out. Joe came in the kitchen to ask if I had something to settle his stomach. He said it was so rough on the flight over that he was afraid he'd lose his breakfast and was looking forward to being on the ground. He was sure he could hold the contents of his stomach after Colin turned to tell him the lake lay just over the hill." He was so low I thought he was going to land but I didn't see any lake and all I could see was trees going past and to me it looked like we were below them. The steep angle of the plane kept me from seeing past the pilot and when he cut the power and dropped down onto the water, all I could think of was I hope that young pilot values his life as much as I do mine or does he prefer to live in the next world?"

Joe had all the trophies he came to hunt and he was the last hunter for the season at Wolf Lake so he was still talking about riding out to the highway when the boys took the horses out. Bud had told him it could be a three to five day tough trip. While Joe was sitting in the kitchen drinking coffee and sharing his concern and trying to decide on what he was going to do, I told him I could sympathize with him because I pretty much had that same feeling on my first trip over the hill with the trees going past the wings then the pilot throttling back to allow just enough RPMs to keep from stalling, he dropped down on to the lake but I had the advantage of confidence in the pilot from the many flights with him. Joe asked my opinion, I didn't hesitate to recommend he fly back out because the air was smooth and he would enjoy the scenic flight. He took my word for it and thanked his pilot, after landing on the highway, then apologized for his unfair opinion of that young pilot.

There was another time, again when Colin was the pilot. He had a hunter from the east with him and on the way back from the highway to Wolf Lake, Colin flew up a canyon in the sheep hills to check on a spike camp. He wanted to see if the hunters and guides had their sheep trophies and were ready to return to base camp or needed more groceries. If they gave him a signal for groceries or were ready, he could tell his dad to send an air drop or send the horses up there to bring them in. When telling me about it in the kitchen this man said "Flying in your high mountains is more scary than walking. Do they land an airplane up there to let a hunter out for sheep? If they do I'll walk and climb up for my ram."

"No way could you entice either of our pilots to land our Super Cub up there in those sheep hills. I hope you didn't misunderstand Colin's reason for flying over that camp. He should have told you what he planned to do and why. I do all the correspondence and I'm sure I told you we set out spike camps in the areas you will be hunting. You ride horses back to this camp, it is supplied for the many days you will be there for the stay and from that camp, you, your guide and packer climb the mountain. The airplane is for transportation from the highway to here and to our base camp" I answered. He was satisfied.

Why is Bud always out of camp leaving me to entertain and answer questions thrown at me faster than I can answer them. Maybe these guys just like to be in my kitchen drinking coffee and eating pie.

There are times during the hunting seasons that something different than expected will happen. Bud flew over a spike camp to see if Mr. Atlee had his grizzly bear and was ready to be moved to a moose hunting camp. He circled the tent camp twice and there was no one in sight around the area. On the second fly-over a hand was waving from the stove pipe hole in the tent. He circled and again he was greeted by the waving hand. Thinking there was an emergency and wondering why there was no other sign of distress (knowing Bud would soon be flying over them,) he was real concerned. There was no place close he could land. He had to find out what had happened to the hunter or his guide. After selecting a landing sight he landed and walked an hour through tangled under brush to reach the camp. Both men were sitting out in the sunshine when he got there. Seems Mr. Atlee had shot at a grizzly bear but missed, then fell in the creek they were crossing, after he changed to dry clothes they were tired and hungry. They had just sat down to eat when Bud flew over and the guide's excuse was Bud wouldn't see a bear hide stretched out so he'd know they were going to stay in camp a while longer. "What in the hell kind of a hand signal was that?" Bud asked the very embarrassed guide.

I was the cook in Cotton Wood camp and didn't hear about that happening until later. I forgot to ask what Bud's reaction was. I'm sure I can guess correctly, unless he added some words I hadn't heard. I was told Mr. Atlee and his guide, Freddy, stayed until he got his grizzly. Freddy somewhat redeemed himself when his hunter collected a very nice grizzly bear and a trophy moose. They had left Wolf Lake before I returned and was glad I wasn't around to hear Bud fume about the chance he had taken when landing the plane where he did and the time spent walking over and back again. I noticed Freddy wasn't part of our crew on future hunts.

One year we had a doctor from Ohio booked for a Dall sheep and a grizzly bear hunt. Our outfit was recommended to him by a client on the hunt with us the previous year. This doctor wrote that he was in top condition and exercising faithfully. Bud was free to be his guide on this hunt while Colin did the flying. When the man arrived Bud was sceptical, he felt the man wasn't in as good physical condition as he thought he was, so he took him on the bear hunt first. Bud thought it was going to be an easy hunt where the grizzly was grazing on berry bushes on an open slope. Crossing the wobbly tundra humps was a new experience for the doctor and he'd have to keep stopping to catch his breath. It was a long day that should not have taken half that time but he had a real decent bear hide for the effort. The next morning Bud asked him if he was ready to climb the sheep hills. With his high powered binoculars, Bud showed him some Dall rams high on the crags of the mountain across from camp. He told Bud he now realized he was not in condition to climb our mountains. He had no idea they would be so vertical and the rams so high up. "I'll just stay in camp and rest for a few days and it's okay if you want to go out with another party." Bud was happy to oblige.

This pleasant man was content to spend the rest of his hunt in camp with me. He spent most of the day in the kitchen, asking questions and just visiting when he wasn't reading the books I had. The stories he told of his work in the hospital were interesting and he said his nurses advised him not to be climbing mountains in Alaska but to be sure to shoot a grizzly bear or they would send him back next year. He was contented with his bear kill and happy to be in a camp as comfortable as ours. He said it was a real vacation for him to be away from the telephones and constant sick people. For the price he was paying for his hunt he could have been staying in a luxury hotel. I felt obligated to entertain him although I was behind schedule with all my other duties. I knew he was a heart specialist in a big hospital, but it amazed me to see how often he smoked! Bud had told him he couldn't smoke when they were after game because an animal can smell smoke a long ways away and would disappear. I asked him one day what he told his patients about smoking.

"I tell them to stop," he answered laughing.

Back at the ranch after hunting season one year Bud wanted me to come look at a strange sight that puzzled him. He had come across it when he was looking for dead trees to haul in for firewood. During the summer he had to shoot an old horse that somebody gave him. The poor animal was awfully skinny but Bud thought he could fatten it up by feeding good hay and grain all winter. Twice it was down and couldn't get back up, Bud could see it was in worse shape than he thought so rather than let it suffer he put it out of its misery, then hauled the carcass quite a distance from the road and house way back in the woods. All summer long we had been seeing a sow grizzly with two cubs and he was sure they would find it and have a feast. Most likely they were the ones that did find it but he couldn't figure out how the four hoofs were left setting just like the horse had walked out of them. We never did figure that one out. I would like to have been a little bird in a tree watching the cubs playing with bones that were scattered in all directions, and maybe just playfully set those hoofs in the order they were left, just to confuse us.

It was the year before that grizzly and her two cubs showed up at the ranch that another bear left its muddy paw prints and slobbers on the low kitchen window trying to see inside. Then it must have gone to the small cabin and batter a window out. Bud had stored his big game trophies in the cabin while building a Trophy room. The bear didn't do any further damage and Bud thinks that when it came face to face with that big white polar bear face looking at it, thinking it was seeing a ghost, it left and we never saw it or its tracks around after that.

I think the term flunkie fits me well, beings I am a bush pilot's wife. No matter how busy I was with my projects or wifely duties, if husband needed two extra hands with his projects and I was the only one handy, I'd often find myself in a position when I'd prefer to be some place else. I wasn't as confident in my ability to handle the project he had delegated to me, as he was. I have asked myself many times why am I the only one around just at the right time? A few more situations like both times I helped him put an airplane in the water and I'll be surprised if I don't have ulcers!

At the ranch one spring, Bud had finished changing the skis on the Super Cub to pontoons and was pushing it down to the lake with the bulldozer in preparation of placing it in the water. He came to the house for lunch while waiting for the man who was supposed to come early to help make the change from skis to floats, then get it in the water so they could go fishing. It was late in the afternoon Bud decided the man wasn't coming so I was elected to help him. The water in the lake was low and that left a high bank that I thought should have been cut down with the dozer before pushing the plane over and into the lake. "It's okay," he told me when I suggested he wait until the morrow and his friend would be there to help him.

"Okay, it's your airplane," I said as we walked down to the floatplane base. I was hanging on to the metal handle attached to the fuselage near the "Tail-Feathers" and my responsibility was to hang on and keep the plane from nosing over as he pushed it over the bank into the water. The handle wasn't wide enough that I could hold with both hands, I only had a hand and a half hold. As he was pushing the plane over the bank and at an angle I was sure it would nose over, I could feel it trying to lift me off my feet, the metal handle was cutting into my fingers and I couldn't decide which would be worse, let go or go over with the airplane. Bud couldn't hear me yell above the noise of the dozer engine and I wasn't sure if he could see over the angle of the tipping plane and was pushing it beyond the point of no return. I was lifted to my toes right at the second the plane balanced and settled in the water.

"I think it would have taken less time to cut the bank down than it would have had the Cub gone on its nose," I told him while murmuring about my hurting fingers.

I was reminded of another time when the Piper J-3 was parked on a river bank in early spring and we were camped over night some distance away. In the morning the river had gone way down leaving the airplane high and dry on the river bank. It was on floats and Bud was too impatient to get it back in the water to wait for help, or face being stranded there for no telling how long. His method of getting it back in the water was for me to stand at the end of one float and he at he other and rock the light plane, inching it into the water and if it tipped too far forward we were to jump on the tail end of the float to keep it from nosing over. I didn't understand how we were to get it into the water, or how we could have pulled it back to solid ground. His calculated risks were better than mine and I was relieved when his method worked. He then explained how the length and weight of the pontoons balanced the airplane and it would tip just so far before going on over. I am thinking how embarrassed he would have been had his method not worked and could it have been called an incident, an accident or an uncontrolled landing?

There was that embarrassing time when his calculated risk ended up being an expensive incident. I use the term accident. He had landed on Tanada Lake in late November when the ice should have been thick enough to hold the Super Cub on wheels. An experienced pilot knows how to test the ice by touching down softly on the ice then flying around to look at the tracks. If water was in the tracks then he knows best not to land with wheels on the plane. Bud landed fairly close to shore and the plane no more than settled on the ice when it dropped into the lake with only the wings out of the water! He had always told me to give him time to walk back before I called anyone to look for him. This trip he planned to fly up to Tanada Lake, unload some supplies and come right back to the ranch. The flying weather was no problem so when he wasn't back the next day I asked our friend Cleo McMahan to check on him. Cleo flew low over the cabin to yell to me Bud was walking out. It was no surprise to me that he was walking back but I had a few hours to wonder why. Could he have possibly wrecked the airplane? He was an experienced pilot, so I thought. This accident is published in detail in the book, *Wind on the Water*.

There was only one time I remember being unduly worried when two pilots were long overdue and I was seriously planning to drive out from the ranch to locate a pilot to go look for them. Colin got in at the tail end of the era when aerial wolf hunting was legal. Now he was the pilot and his dad the gunner. I'd be amused with Colin's stories about their day flying together on their return home. Bud had been in the cockpit for so many years it was hard for him to put his complete attention to watching the wolf below and let the pilot do all the maneuvering for position. Bud's advice to all the gunners he has had with him in past years was: "trust the pilot or don't go flying with him. I have to trust you not to shoot us down instead of the wolf you are shooting at." Now he was receiving those same instructions.

Bud put total trust in his son's skill as a pilot but he couldn't resist looking at the terrain ahead instead of below and then if he missed a good shot the second time around, or maybe it would be a third time if they had that chance, Colin would turn and ask if he wanted in the cockpit. They were both beaming. Colin remarked that he finally had his dad trained and he redeemed himself by two direct kills on two overhead passes.

All the years Bud aerial wolf hunted he was well prepared for cold weather overnight camping as well as most any emergency, Colin had these skills also. They had always returned in a reasonable length of time and I had no reason to worry. This time they were gone two long days and one bright moonlight night. Both days were clear and calm with twenty below temperatures, good days to be flying. With the full moonlight on the white snow, they could easily have flown home. Due to previous commitments at home, they had planned to fly for a few hours and then be back. I'm sure I would have not been concerned had they planned to do some hunting, I knew they were enjoying a comfortable camp under a big spruce tree with plenty of wood for a bonfire, good tent, warm sleeping bags and plenty to eat.

On arrival home late the second day, I rushed to the plane the minute the plane slid to a stop in front of the garage. Their story was they had picked up the tracks of a pack of wolves chasing a cow moose and her calf. They were not sure where they would be the next day so they decided to camp and continue looking early the next morning. "Didn't you get that Union Express letter I sent to let you know we were staying here overnight ?" Bud asked, trying to be funny. I held my nose after one sniff of the stinking wolf he held on his lap. I then ran to the house to get the camera. Darn ! I was too late for a picture. He was to eager to get out of the cramped position he was sitting in. They had skinned one wolf with a black hide and using it as a seat cushion, with one wolf setting upright in back of him with its front paws on Bud's shoulders, and a huge gray wolf on his lap with one of its front legs up around his neck. The smell was awful, but would have made a precious picture.

"If you think it smelled bad from outside the airplane just imagine what it smelled like in the cockpit." Colin said while helping pull the third one out and carrying it to the garage. It wasn't advisable to get down wind of either of those guys. Sometimes I wonder if the excitement of the chase is as much fun as the work they left themselves in for.

When I got back to the garage with my camera they had the two big dog wolves stretched out side by side on a tarp in preparation for the skinning job. They were identical in size and gray markings, Bud estimated they weighed close to two hundred pounds each. They lay there with ears up, lips back exposing vicious looking bared fangs like they were ready to jump up and tear you to pieces. I was happy to know their stomachs weren't filled with baby moose calf meat. Mama moose had her calf with her for at least a while longer.

"We just as well get to work while waiting for the fire to warm it up in here," Bud said to Colin. "She won't even let us in her kitchen to eat until we finish this job and take a shower. Before she had her nice kitchen she didn't used to be so particular. Strange what a difference in attitude about modern kitchens." He was right. Tolerating those stinking carcasses was a thing of the past for me.

Colin's sense of humor surfaced and he said to his dad while I was in the garage, "a pilot I know made points with his wife when returning two whole days late and telling her, as cute as you are when you're mad, you would have no problem getting a new husband who'd always be home on time. Are you sure you wasn't happy that I'd not be coming home?" He left when things started flying in his direction.

I was flying with Bud one time and saw the blood covered snow where a pack of wolves had killed a cow moose. Reading the story of the struggle in the snow, they were eating on her while her intestines were dragging as she ran fighting to her last breath. After that scene of an education on the cruelty of nature, I wasn't sorry to know a wolf died suddenly from a shot from an airplane. Yet I always enjoyed hearing them howling in the wilds. We never made it a policy to shoot any of the many wolves we had now roaming in our area, or the ten that lived close to the ranch.

Chapter Ten

The Final Chapter to an Adventure Filled Life

J anuary of 1964 Bud, Colin and I flew out to Detroit to purchase a new Chrysler station wagon we ordered direct from the factory. While in the lower 48, we toured all places of interest, visited our families in the various places then drove the Alcan Highway back to Alaska. We hadn't been back home long when the big earth quake happened on Good Friday, March 1964.

Bud had been impatient to fly the airplane, and made an excuse to fly up to Tanada Lake. I was in the kitchen when the dishes, pots and pans were crashing to the floor, and pictures falling off the walls. Colin was out in the yard, and yelled for me to come look at the tripod, we watched the chain hoist swaying back and forth. It didn't take me long to realize it had to be a real shaker of a quake the way that chain hoist was swinging with the tripod almost falling over, we could see the ground roll. The station wagon was rolling back and forth, even with the brakes set. To feel the ground roll under our feet was a new sensation, and we didn't know which direction to get away from it but then it stopped before we had to make that decision. Colin went to see what damage was done in the garage and I started cleaning up the glass and broken dishes, wondering what was happening with Bud, and the airplane. Was the plane setting on the ice at Tanada Lake, did the ice break up? Then I'm thinking he most likely was in the air and didn't even know there was an earth quake. From the kitchen window I didn't see any ice broken up on the lake.

It wasn't long until I heard the Super Cub return and land on Cobb Lake. He stated he had landed on Tanada Lake, out from the shore, and started to walk away from the plane to investigate what looked like something had been killed, judging by the bloody snow. He said he hadn't walked ten feet, when the ice started moving and water started spurting through the ice, slapping the underside of the wing. When he saw the ice from the lake piling up on the shore, he knew it had to be an earthquake, and best he get the plane back in the air. The engine started right up. (It hadn't been setting long enough to cool off.) Returning to Cobb Lake, flying over other lakes he saw the ice breaking and piling up on shores. In route home he saw two moose staggering around trying to walk. We heard of other pilots who were in the air, and didn't know there was an earthquake, trying to figure out why the moose they saw were staggering, and could hardly keep their balance. Strange the way the ground rolled, while the ice on Cob lake didn't even crack.

It was days before we got any word about how badly Anchorage was damaged. Glennallen radio station; KCAM, was the only news and it was pretty skimpy. Some time later when I took the station wagon in to Anchorage, the roof of the Chevrolet garage was on top of a show case full of new cars. They looked real flat.

Ten years after we moved to Eagle Trail Ranch we moved into our modern two story log house. Bud had hauled the milled logs from a saw mill just across the border in Canada. The size of the house we built, required about five trips. Occasionally we had help with the building project but it was mostly Bud's dedicated hard work and myself as his handy man. Moving into a three bedroom house from a two room cabin was real progress. The trophy room with a stone fireplace was to come later. We had installed two Witte generators for power, also a well drilled before we started building just to be sure of having water; we did get good water and plenty of it. Now I had my log home in Alaska with a fireplace even though it took twenty years. It was a promise he made before we left San Diego and I threatened him I wouldn't go otherwise. The possibility of failure never entered Bud Conkle's head. It may take awhile but he would never give up and often quoted the Sea Bee's slogan; "The impossible just takes longer."

After these many years in Alaska I realize what it is the men with adventure in their heart have felt in the lure of Alaska that gets in their blood. The long dark days are no hindrance to them because there is always work to do, machinery and equipment to repair and places to fly. They feel equal to the challenge of cold metal, cold gas, cold engines to start, wood for the fires and meat for the table. The airplane to take in to a hanger someplace for the annual inspection and that is a time to run into other pilots and socialize. I wonder about how some of these pilot's wives have absorbed the same euphoria—the love of the land—the challenges, etc. from our husbands or from our own experiences. I would never want to leave Alaska. I have flown with my husband and my son on many flights over snow capped mountains, snow covered winter lands, seen wolves running flat out ahead of the shadow of our airplanes, moose contentedly feeding, belly deep, in lake bottoms, glaciers shining in winter and summer suns, northern spruce beneath us standing tall in feudal groups, soft green tundra looking like a deep pile rug—every beautiful view from the air that Alaska has to offer.

The trilogy about life in the bush country, the unpredictable people, their harsh lives, their resilience is something that so many Dudes in the Lower 48 cannot understand or why anyone would want to live here in this beautiful state.

I never wearied of the stories of the old prospectors, hunting guides, pioneers who were here ahead of us. They had stories to tell and it's sad that soon nothing would be left of their life except those stories. With the passage of time the old ones who lived them and their stories also would be faded from memory. I was always anxious to get back to my notes and writing before they too drifted away in the wind.

Harry was old when we met him. He had been a packer and horse wrangler for a big game outfitter and the stories he'd tell us were stranger than fiction; true stories that were not embellished, of an early time when Alaska was sparsely settled. He was a gifted story teller and I was sad I didn't have a tape recorder to record them as he told them. His bear tales were endless, his and others he knew of. I liked to watch him light his pipe with a sulfur match (we called them kitchen matches.) His cheeks pulling in like bellows, smoke leaking out the corners of his mouth, he'd continue on with the story he was telling. Soon he'd relinquish his pipe long enough to tell another story unless it was time for him to go home. His was a voice out of a colorful time and place. His physical health and energy as well as his memory, belied his 80 years of age. One of the stories Harry told was when the Tok Highway was under construction and a road camp was close to Slana. The crew was boarded there and the camp had a full time cook. When the breakfasts were over the cook tossed what pancakes were left, to a two year old grizzly that came to the door regularly for his handouts after the crew left. This had been going on for some time. One morning there was no pancakes left over. The bear was waiting patiently and obvious it wasn't going to leave without its pancakes. The cook didn't want to make more so thinking to discourage it, he wrapped a flat stone in a stale piece of bread and tossed it to the bear like he had been doing every morning. The bear caught it like it was expecting the usual feed, chomped onto the stone, let out a deep growl and headed for the door of the canvas cook tent. The cook exited out the back under the canvas and up a near by tree. When the crew showed up for lunch, the cook was still up the tree, with no lunch ready! The foreman arrived in time to rescue the cook not only from the bear but also the angry hungry crew.

Charlie Evens was another of my favorite old timers whose infrequent visits I'd enjoyed. He was an old prospector in fair condition, with a patina of age and hardships on his lined face. He had an aversion to civilization, he had told us, so hc moved out to a very remote area, as far away as he could get from the "electrified hysteria" of the city life he had left. Bud and I had chanced to meet him on one of our trips when scouting game country. He had a mining claim and it was obvious it didn't produce great wealth for all the hard work he put into digging for whatever gold was in the sand. He was happy in the rustic log cabin he had built. The wild life around him was all the companionship he needed, so he said. If weather and landing conditions were good, there were times I'd go with Bud in the airplane and we'd land on the overflow on the river near his cabin to see what he needed in the way of groceries etc. and especially just to check on him with time to chat awhile. He too had interesting stories to tell. One side of his face was badly scarred from a close encounter with a wolf that had caught him at a disadvantage.

"Well I wasn't a good looking guy to start with," he said and went on to tell about that day when he shot the wolf and thought it was dead. They had a wrestling match in the snow and he came close to being the one who ended up dead.

I was always curious about these old boys' earlier life before thy came to Alaska, because most of the ones I knew did come from some place else and had their reasons why. Some never tell you but I had known Charlie some time before I got an opportune time to tease him about maybe a romance that went sour. His terse answer to that was; "I was married but we had lost the habit of one another and weren't able to reacquire it again, I didn't miss her that much anyhow."

There was an occasional time when Charlie walked many miles from his cabin to Wolf Lake. Maybe he was lonesome but didn't admit it. Some times he wanted Bud to get things for him at a store when he was out to the highway and air drop it to him. The times Bud flew over his cabin they had a signal for certain things. When Charlie was nearing the time when he knew he wasn't going to be able to live out where he couldn't get around well enough to take care of himself anymore, he signed a paper deeding his cabin to Bud. He didn't have title to the land and then when it ended up within the Wrangell St. Elias National Park it didn't belong to us anymore. Charlie didn't last very long after he went into the Pioneers Home.

Bud scattered his ashes over his cabin area. A few years later I was with Bud when he landed on the ice near the deserted, decaying cabin. The roof sagging, window batted out most likely by a bear, the door agape and the ground wearing away by the encroaching river. Like most of the old ones who are gone now. I think Charlie too would have preferred his life had ended right there, but he didn't have that choice. I wonder if he remembered laughing and telling me one time when the conversation was about how easy it was to get yourselves killed living out in the boonies, "I came into this world crying and I intend to go out laughing, let others do the crying."

There was an old Native, Chief John, from the village on the Nabesna River, who came to visit us when we were living at Tanada Lake. He died before I had gained his confidence and he took the stories with him to the grave. He had lived most of his life there and was buried there. His bones will nourish the soil along with those of his ancestors. But there were others who knew their histories, their traditions and beliefs. The more time we spent with them the more they would tell us. A young son knew about the Batzulnitas village on the Copper River located where Tanada Creek empties into the Copper. Bud and I had came across a faint trail starting from the Nabesna Road. Curious as usual we followed it to this abandoned village. It had piqued my imagination ever since then and I had flown over it many times to and from Tanada and Cobb lakes. I finally had a chance to go there again with my young son on his new Arctic Cat snowmachine.

Colin had covered about every trail within miles of Eagle Trail Ranch. One very bright full moon light night, he asked if I'd like to ride with him up the Nabesna Road. I was ready in a short time and as we were on the road a few miles up from Slana we saw snow machine trails. "Wonder where that trail goes?" he asked "Let's go have a look," I agreed as it would be an interesting place to see what it looked like from the ground knowing he had also seen it many times from the air.

The village had been abandoned for many years, the few crumbling log cabins and caches echoed with loneliness. Weathered wooden frames of ancient graves, the whitewashed paint pealed and faint, standing guard around young and old erected there by the loved ones buried there also long ago. The skeletons of drying racks and fish wheels over grown with willows and tundra grass. The river relentlessly eating closer to what is still left. In time it too will be forgotten history.

I am pleased to know Colin knows this history and it will be passed on down to his children, my grandchildren and theirs. Those were a special breed. Those early pioneers who mushed the trails, staked their claims, mined for gold, hunted the game, trapped the furs, caught the fish and proved up on the ground where they rest today. There is so much early history in this area we have known; Tanada Lake, the Nabesna Mine, Cobb Lakes and the old Eagle Trail.

I did a lot of the correspondence when booking prospective clients and this was mostly during the winter. I would type the letters Bud wrote to the clients as, like he would say—his hand writing was so bad he couldn't read it himself. As a general rule, the clients preferred getting an answer to their inquiries direct from the outfitter in preference to his wife. After so many letters back and forth I begin to feel I know the man before he arrives. There have been times it was up to me to make the decision if it was okay for the wife to come with him and stay in camp with me while he was hunting. This makes extra work but more times than not, it will be a pleasant time for her, if she is congenial and helpful. The type of woman who likes to go camping and places with her husband. She is charged a set price but can't expect to be waited on. I have ended up with some lasting friendships with a few of these wives.

We were always anxious to have a full hunting season so with every letter of inquiry from prospective hunters I'd sometimes be too eager to sell the hunt and agree the wife can come also. Writing to two doctors from Germany, I was anxious to book them and agreed that Herta could also come. The doctor who was doing the correspondence didn't come right out and say that Herta was his wife but she was coming with them but wasn't going to hunt. He didn't say that she would be staying in camp with me but I was so eager to book those people from Germany, thinking to get references and bookings from future hunters from their country, I agreed she could go to Cottonwood Camp with me. Neither one spoke good English and no one in camp spoke German. Herta was pleasant and easy to please but we hadn't anticipated the doctor insisting she accompany him on his hunts. It soon became obvious she was not his wife. That was none of our business and one is careful not to repeat certain stories in wrong places. What did create a problem was for the guide trying to keep two people quiet when the client did get within shooting range of a trophy Dall ram, then have it disappear because they were paying more attention to each other than to his instructions. The second time that happened Mike, the registered guide, brought them back to camp. One of my duties, talents too, was to smooth over serious situations like this because I was the one who had said they could hunt together. Bud was the other doctor's guide for his sheep hunt. My solution was to send Mike up to Bud's camp and if it was agreeable with the client then Mike stay and go with him, having Bud come back and take this man on his hunt. I had a long day keeping two people amused when we couldn't understand each other.

Bud made it clear he would put forth every effort to get him within shooting range of a real big ram but only one person would climb the mountain with him. If he wanted Herta to go that was okay with him or he would go and she would stay in camp with me. Herta, Jim the horse wrangler and I had an enjoyable time for three days in camp. We picked berries, hiked up canyons, rode the horses and amused ourselves reading or glassing the sheep hills. Late afternoon of the third day while we were back in camp, five shots echoed across the valley. Like a shot Herta and Jim grabbed their packboards and took off up the mountain in the direction Bud and Dr. Foss had taken. I stayed in camp to prepare dinner.

There was another year when I did the correspondence that I booked a man and wife hunting together. Sounded good in the letters we exchanged but she didn't make herself popular with the guides, the other hunters in camp, or with me and my helper in the kitchen. It was bad enough that she always had to get a bigger game animal than her husband but she also wanted a bigger trophy than the other men came back to camp with. In the kitchen she wanted Mildred and I to treat her like she was the queen bee. The woman's husband was such an easy going, pleasant man so I tolerated her. Otherwise I'd have treated her like I was sorely tempted to do.

I spent many hours in the winter months putting the 35 MM color slides in proper order. We both took a lot of slides and 16MM movies to show on trips to the Lower 48 while booking hunts. We were getting invitations from our clients to come visit them in the States. They would invite their friends to come see the hunting pictures and maybe book a hunt with us. After a couple of winters of this Bud was getting well known in hunting circles. We were catering to more hunters each year. This required more guides, more horses, with a lot more work for me in the kitchen also managing to keep more groceries in camp. I had help now and then when I could find some one willing to cook and wash dishes without all the modern conveniences that "Bush-Life" offers.

I was at a Guide Board meeting with Bud and one of the noted pilot-guide's wife and I were listening to the stories and credit all the attending pilots and guides were getting and we decided it was about time their wives got some of the credit.

The romantic image of the Northern Bush Pilot, big game hunting guide and outfitter has been around for a long time. But what about their wife? She is the other half of the business. We decided it was about time we got some of the credit!

While showings pictures to the hunting crowd; there was always an admiring crowd. Bud was a convincing story teller and had developed a knack of glorifying himself and his life style with his audience eager to hear it all. He could impress his audience with his narrow escape from grizzly bears, a mad moose cow, flying stories and his ability to handle almost every situation. For the most part, his stories were all true happenings (with a little embellishment now and then) and a bit evasive with the truth when his version was more exciting. The polar bear movies and the stories that went with them were different than most of these audiences had been exposed to and it did sound dangerous and exciting. He was lapping up the adoration of the ladies in the crowd who thought they had found a new hero. Sometimes one of the ladies in the audience would say to me; "My what an exciting life you live, then ask me if I hunted and shot those animals too and did I fly the airplane? When I told them what those glamorous pilots and guides wives did, they would answer, "Oh, I wouldn't like that kind of life."

I would help Bud at the projector when he'd show the 35MM sides at the various trophy rooms in some very expensive homes. Since I knew where all the slides belonged in their individual slots I had some handy, and at times I'd slip them in when I'd find myself being completely ignored, with my vanity dictating to me that I should have been included in this glory, I'd slip in a slide of the outhouse, or me over the scrub board washing his blood soaked clothes after butchering and packing wild game, especially me hanging clothes on an outdoor clothes line, cooking on a wood stove with eight men waiting at the table, hauling and heating buckets of water, on the wood range and the oval galvanized bath tub.

Oh-Yea! The life of a bush pilot wife.

It sure disillusioned those women in the audiences, some of whose husbands had hunted with our outfit and went home bragging about the meals I cooked and what a great hunting camp we had and the country we hunted in. Those wives didn't realize that those delicious meals I cooked for their husbands; sheep steaks cooked on a grill in a spike camp, bread and pies baked in a wood stove in base camp, tasted so good to them because they were hungry from all the outdoor activity. I didn't get a chance to show my side of our glamourous life too often. Bud made sure those slides weren't included for most of our showings.

I got bragging rights with my sourdough pancakes and was pleased with the compliments from the men at the breakfast table. Then one morning during a busy hunting season, a pilot friend was helping Bud with the flying, I was too interested in the stories being told at the breakfast table and forgot to put the soda in the sour dough. I noticed the questioning look on the guys faces but Bud and Walt (the other pilot) didn't eat theirs. Walt, had said he didn't like sourdough bread or pancakes. I had said I was sure he would like these. I think it may have cured him of ever wanting to try them again.

I was more diplomatic than Bud when it came to handling situations such as when a client and his guide were not compatible and they would complain to me. Feelings could get hurt if you took a guide from one client and gave him a different one. I could always talk them into being happy about the change. I was a sympathetic listener to the boys working for us and helped smooth hurt feelings if they got a chewing out from the boss if a horse came in with saddle sores or the tack wasn't properly taken care of. I had salve for the horses sores as well as medicines for cuts and bruises of the crew. All the doctors we catered to always brought along their supply of medicines then left it with me and how to use it when they left.

Dr. Jackson, from South Carolina, was a favorite of ours in camp. He had made two hunts with us and said he would like to make another in a year or so. But his wife wasn't going to agree to let him go hunting any more. She wanted to go to Paris and other places. He said he didn't mind her going but he wasn't interested in any of those places. If his hunting buddies in their tent after supper, were drinking and the stories too raunchy, he would come to the kitchen. I'd get us each a cup of coffee and listen to him tell of his work at the hospital and his patients. It was obvious he was a dedicated doctor and had the patients interests at heart. I told him that in my opinion he needed the outdoor relaxation from his strenuous duties at a busy hospital.

From her point of view as a doctors wife, maybe she feels she has been home in past years tending the home fires while he spent most of his time at the hospital. I was tempted to offer my opinion that he should go hunting regardless. As a after thought, that was one time I didn't voice an opinion when asked. I was thinking maybe he would tell her that and then he wouldn't be hunting anymore. If he went hunting again it wasn't with us, I would be sorry I hadn't told him how I felt about it when he had asked me. The way the majority of the men who were under constant pressures enjoyed their time away from telephones and business stress, they departed for home relaxed and ready to get back to work.

At least there was no stress in my work. If I was irritated or something bothering me, as soon as I finished my work, I'd go out and sit on a log by the lake and watch the ducks swimming contentedly and often in September, the wolves were howling in the distance. One September we had an early freeze and I was out watching reflections on the ice. The ducks had left early, all but one. Just at dusk this lone duck, spotting a wet margin along a crack in the ice, landed with a thud and sat seemingly stunned, or was it too tired to travel farther? It couldn't get airborne without open water and was too far out on thin ice for me to try to rescue it. I was feeling sorry for the duck and trying to figure out a way to help it but at almost too dark to see, an eagle swooped down and scooped it up. It made me sad after having a good day myself but then the eagle had to eat too.

Time passes and things change. I was pleased with the decision Bud made that it was time to cut down on some of our work. Time to do a few things we had talked about doing but never enough time. Our neighbors at Grizzly Lake Lodge bought our cabins (by now had major improvements), the horses and grazing rights at Wolf Lake. Bud still maintained areas to hunt Dall sheep in an exclusive guiding area, where he could take a select few moose and bear hunters. This left me more time at home in my big new house. Time to hang pictures, unpack boxes that had been stored since we moved from Tanada Lake and no place for them in a small homestead cabin.

Besides packing everything I wanted to keep from the Wolf Lake cabin, one of my last important tasks was to keep an eye on the Super Cub, anchored in the cove just out of my sight, so

I frequently had to leave my kitchen work and take a look. Bud had left to drive the weasel out to the highway, load it on the truck, take it to the ranch and Colin would fly him back to Wolf Lake in his Cessna 180. So it would be two days or more before they were due back. I had to pack in such a way that what I was taking would fit in behind me, around me and on me for my last trip from here in the Super Cub. The 180 had to take off from the short lake with a very light load, lift off conditions were just right.

I had to keep a close eye on the bull moose that stayed in the lake and didn't want to leave. It either resented the airplane tethered in one of its favorite feeding spots or just maybe thought it was a rival. I could see it from the kitchen where I was working but if it wasn't in sight I'd go out to see where it was. Sometimes it would shake its massive horns at the plane and I'd wave my arms and yell. I was startled when it lowered his head and started walking toward me. I ran for the cabin. He would be gone for awhile and then return. Finally three shots in rapid succession from my 300 Magnum rifle sent it galloping off into the trees, he didn't return. I was getting desperate thinking what those big horns could do to the fabric covered wings and fuselage and what would Bud's reaction be when he returned and saw the Super Cub in tatters and a dead bull moose in the lake. However, everything was under control by the time the men returned.

On our last flight from Wolf Lake to Eagle Trail Ranch we had a passenger. There would not have been room for it if it had been any larger. I climbed in the tandem seat and a big black horse fly flew in the open side door while Bud was standing alongside waiting for me to fasten my seat belt so he could place my sleeping bag on my lap and gear on both sides of me, (it didn't matter that I couldn't see out. I had flown that route many times). Bud didn't spend much time trying to chase the elusive fly back out.

"Okay, if you are determined to bum a ride I'll dump you some place and you can find your own way back!" Bud said while poking things in where ever it would fit.

With all the experience I have had over the years packing things to fit in a J-3 and a Super Cub, pickup, station wagon and horse panniers (baskets,) it wasn't surprising that it all fit and met with the pilot's approval for weight. Most Super Cub pilots can judge the amount of weight they are loading just by lifting it.

On our way home that fly circled the cockpit a few times, once around the pilot's head, dodging my attempts to swat it from my cramped position, then settled some place out of my sight and flew home with us. When the plane settled at its parking place and the motor shut off, Bud opened the side door and the fly flew out and away without a thank you for the free ride.

Those past years at Tanada Lake and then at Wolf Lake had gone by fast now that we are settled in one place and I can be home with a dependable car. To start with we had a CB radio, later a radio telephone for communication.

It had been a tremendous responsibility for me those past years to make some of the decisions I was faced with at various times when I was in those isolated places with no way to send word out or get a message to me in a real emergency. I think I felt equal to the challenge at that time. It must have been the same with those other wives of other professional Bush Pilots, who also lived in isolated homesteads and hunting camps. Most live in grizzly country with kids to raise. No modern home with telephone communication until a later date, more often than not, after the kid were grown up and departed.

Late fall of 1984 when the hunting season was over for another year, we were finalizing our plans for another drive out to the lower 48 to visit some of our past clients as well as relatives and friends. We made no definite time that we had to be back. I had completed a white safari hunting jacket that I had made for Bud to wear on this trip. It was made from tanned elk hides bleached white. It was a real professional looking jacket and Bud was pleased I had put forth the effort to have it finished by the time we were leaving on this trip. It was a classy looking jacket and made me wonder if I was in the wrong business. I could make these and sell them. I had made him a two-toned leather vest with fringe and conches, he liked it and he wore it constantly.

When Bud was trapping beavers I'd think about all those expensive beaver coats and parkas I'd see some lucky women wearing and wondered if I'd ever be lucky enough to coax Bud out of enough to make my own parka. Just wishful thinking because we always needed the money and had to sell the pelts. I was satisfied with a lovely muskrat parka with a beaver ruff.

We had purchased a second hand fifth wheel trailer house that was in almost perfect condition, this time we traveled in leisurely comfort. On returning home in late February 1985 from a month long trip to the Lower-48, our road was blown shut with snow. We had a neighbor take us in to the house with his snow machine. Bud built a fire in the garage while I built the fire in the wood range in the kitchen. Later he would get the furnace going to heat the rest of the house and then activate the thawed water system. Everything had been shut down and drained before we left on our trip.

The young couple living in the homestead cabin had their own living quarters and didn't need the garage. They didn't know when we'd be returning. Bud was impatient to get the road bladed open so he first cranked the Witte light plant then planned to get the bulldozer running. The generator, having stood so long in a cold garage, was reluctant to start and Bud was determined to keep cranking on it until it did start. It didn't have an electric start, just a hand crank. Greg Slaseman, the young fellow living in the cabin, was in the garage and strong enough to have taken turns cranking on the generator but Bud thought he had to do it. He was too impatient to wait over another day and let the equipment warm up a bit and with the barrel stove producing heat all night it would have started a lot easier and I'm sure the Caterpillar dozer also.

I was melting snow and looking in the cupboards for something to cook for lunch and looking around in the frozen canned goods supply to start thawing meat and vegetables for our dinner, when Greg came to the house and said best I come to the garage, Bud was doubled over and in serious pain. Seems Bud had made two pulls on the pony-engine (a small attached engine that is used to preheat and crank over the main engine.) Bud said he felt something happen in his chest. He was sitting doubled over close to the stove and said he thought it best we get him to the doctor. The doctor was eighty-miles away at Glennallen. Greg and I zipped him up in a sleeping bag on Greg's snow machine and took him over to the Heart D Ranch, then borrowed their station wagon. (Our pickup was still attached to the house trailer.) Asked them to call the ambulance from Glennallen, we would meet the ambulance in route. He died in my arms before the ambulance reached us! At the hospital the doctor said it was a massive heart attack, so severe he would have been an invalid the rest of his life had they been able to save him.

Bud was steeled with the knowledge that hard work solves everything. He was strong and had worked hard all his life but he hadn't allowed for the fact he had been living pretty soft and without the constant exercise he was used to, plus all the rich dinners those people had fed us where we had visited, these past months. He simply over did it this time doing what he had been used to doing for so long. Knowing how determined he was about everything, I was under the impression he would say he wasn't going to die and he wouldn't. He didn't have a choice this time. He would have been a miserable man spending the rest of his life in a wheel chair—looking to the sky.

LeNora with a lake trout she caught in Tanada Lake.

LeNora and Colin with a lake trout fishing through the ice on Tanada Lake.

LeNora wearing the blue velvet parka she made.

An 18-month old baby in a sheep hunting camp.

The pickup and 5th wheel trailer we drove to the Lower-48.

Colin in berry patch.

A baby, a cat, and a dog ready to cross the lake to the saw mill.

LeNora fitting and sewing the fabric on the J-3 Cub.

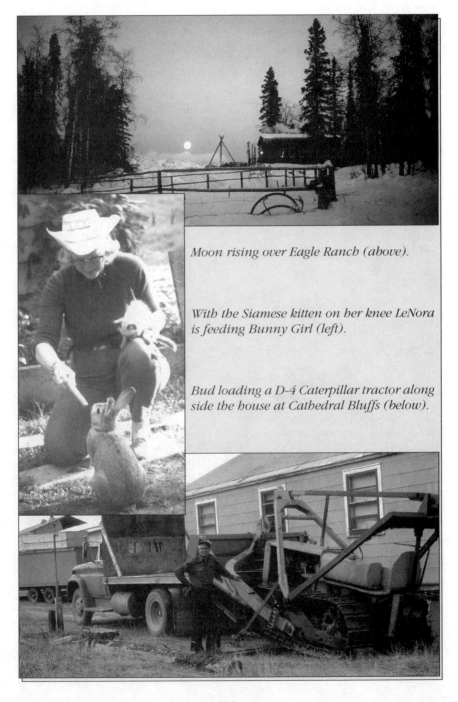

Moon rising over Eagle Ranch (above).

With the Siamese kitten on her knee LeNora is feeding Bunny Girl (left).

Bud loading a D-4 Caterpillar tractor along side the house at Cathedral Bluffs (below).

Chapter Eleven

Daphne McMahan

Daphne Cunningham was born and raised in St Paul, Minnesota, and after she graduated from high school she moved to Seattle, Washington to be near family and relatives. She found a job as a secretary in a lawyer's office. While in Seattle she and her girl friend, hearing about

Daphne and Cleo McMahan.

a shortage of workers in Anchorage, Alaska and high paying wages, applied and were accepted for jobs. She worked as a clerk in a bank and later as secretary for the Fire Control

Service (FCS). It was while she was working at the FCS she met Cleo McMahan.

Cleo was with the Forest Service as a fire control guard at Anchorage. He had started taking flying lessons and bought a Taylor Craft airplane and had soloed in 1941 but was drafted into the US Army, so his flying lessons were put on hold. He then sold his share of the plane. He continued his flight training in Seattle later (until he had his pilot's license), then he was classified as 4F because of a stiff right arm, this disqualified him for military service.

Cleo and Daphne were married in Seattle in 1943. They moved to Fort Yukon where Cleo was working for the FCS. After spending some time in Fort Yukon and Valdez they moved to Meiers Lake at Mile 170 on the Richardson Highway. They had a cabin site there and a bush landing strip. After they had a liveable house on the property, they started a big game hunting business under the name—McMAHAN GUIDE AND FLYING SERVICE. He had passed all the required tests with the Guide Licensing Board and had a registered guide licence for Alaska and now a commercial pilot's license.

While they were living at Meiers, Daphne gave birth to two daughters, and two sons. There was no hospital or doctors within miles of Meiers, so Daphne had to go all the way to Anchorage where their first daughter Susie was born. Then later to Valdez, where Sally was born. When their sons were due, she would stay with friends in Glennallen. At that time here was no hospital in Glennallen. Babies were delivered in a improvised room at the Department of Highways, attended by the doctor who had recently arrived. A hospital was in the process of being built, but some babies didn't wait.

When old enough, the two girls, Susie and Sally, were on correspondence courses for schooling—The Calvert Course from Lincoln, Nebraska. In 1953, the year Chuck was born, they moved to Gakona for the winters. There was a grade school and an airfield there. Gakona was a place with a lot of early Alaska history. It is located alongside the Gakona River and the historic Gakona Lodge.

At the time they moved to Gakona, Ted Lambert, a famous Alaska artist (painter), was living there and was practically their neighbor. It wasn't until later he became famous with his paintings.

Daphne applied for and was accepted for driving the only

Gakona school bus, this meant driving on dangerous winter roads unless school was canceled (with temperature at 50 degrees below zero). When school was out in the spring they moved back to Meiers. The house in Gakona had indoor plumbing and in the late 1950s a flush toilet in contrast to the outhouse and water system at Meiers.

At their home and business at Meiers they had added on rooms as the children arrived and grew. A fifty-five-gallon drum in the rafters over the kitchen stored water pumped from the well, then gravity to the sink, with four pre-schoolers in a home, it takes a lot of water, even if carefully used. For a young lady who had grown up with modern conveniences most of her life, she managed well.

When a school bus was necessary to take the local high school kids to Glennallen high school, she bid, and got the contract. This demanded a much larger passenger bus. She hadn't considered the later models with all those gears and things she wasn't used to in the station wagons she had been driving. At this time (in Alaska's' youth), a CDL (Commercial Drivers Licence) was not required to operate a school bus. This bus was delivered to their home, with no one to instruct her. But that didn't deter her from experimenting on all the back roads. She now felt she was ready to pick up the kids on Monday morning.

All the years she drove that school bus up and down the treacherous Gakona hill (before the section of new highway was built), she had fearful visions of the narrow part of the road close to the edge where it dropped off to the Copper River far below, imagining this bus sliding off the road, after a heavy rain, and her load of children tumbling down into the river. She would contemplate what actions she would be prepared to take to rescue the children. She could swim well, had climbed Mt. Rainier and various outdoor activities, and felt confident she could and would do something! Luckily that disaster never occurred. The new road was widened at that point, and by cutting into the steep bank, a wider shoulder was added. During the construction, however; a different hazard confronted her, a temporary 'switch- back' had been built. Mud at the bottom of the hill, at the curve, required expert handling while the bus was sliding back and forth, trying to end up in the ditch, or into the berm, before she could get it under control. Now she had a bus full of kids laughing and thinking it fun.

Daphne was more inclined to take action than she was to spend time worrying but when Cleo was on a brown bear hunt on the Alaska Peninsula, or a polar bear hunt out from Barrow, when he'd be gone for a month or more. She knew there was no point in worrying. He'd call or show up at home.

There was very few times Cleo was overdue for any length of time and she was pacing the floor not knowing if it was going to be good news, or bad, when she did hear. When he'd be gone for a month or more on the polar bear hunts, it was always weather that kept him grounded with no way to send a message, but he'd call as soon a he could get to a phone. At Meiers they had a high frequency (HF) radio they could keep in touch and Cleo had a very high frequency (VHF & HF) radio in his plane. The only two times he had an accident - once right in his back yard when he set the plane in the trees with minimal damage to the plane - then again with the Cessna on floats, on a lake in one of his hunting camps. He saw he wasn't going to make it over the hill at the end of the lake so he landed back on the lake but ran out of water and couldn't stop, so ran up on the shore. He told the hunter he had with him that it "wasn't-where-he-had-planned-to-land." Neither one was shook up and no serious damage to the plane.

Harley was a licensed pilot now, and with radios in both planes, Daphne didn't have to wait long for any news (good or bad). He flew out to help his dad get the plane back in the water.

Both sons had their pilot's licenses and their own airplanes while they were still young men. Now Daphne had three pilots to worry about when they were missing, or overdue, even though both boys were married at the time of their accidents. Harley had crashed landed his airplane on the side of a mountain and the saying in pilot lingo —"any crash you can walk away from is a good crash!" He limped away from it with a broken ankle, fractured skull, and numerous cuts on his face. While his dad and some of the other pilots were searching for him, he was walking to a hunting camp he knew the location of. To get there he had to swim across the Chistochina River. He had walked many miles to another hunting guide's camp. On arrival — pilot Rocky Keene, flew him to a telephone to tell his dad where he was. Chuck was only missing one long afternoon, and over night, before he was located with his airplane on its back on a lake. Chuck wasn't hurt, but highly embarrassed! He was on wheels and tried to land on a lake free of snow. It was early May and the snow covered ice was soft. His ELT went off. He was located early the next morning.

Daphne was a real business woman and good manager. She knew a good investment and took action when opportunity knocked. She saw the future in a investment in land at Gakona, at the time homesteading was available, and convinced Cleo the possibilities of owning land shouldn't be ignored. Having convinced him, they homesteaded twenty acres where they had their house in Gakona, and one-hundred-twenty-acres on the hill above Gakona. There were no public laundry facilities or showers within miles of Gakona so Cleo and some other man build a small frame building she equipped with two showers, four Speed Queen washers and two dryers. The two daughters, Susie and Sally, earned college money taking care of the 'Bubble Room' for two years.

It was a few years later she saw the advantage of selling land at Gakona and building their home on the hill. First she measured the land where an airstrip could be built before convincing Cleo of this major undertaking. He was dedicated to his flying and guiding business and wasn't too interested in adding more projects. That didn't deter Daphne. After he bulldozed the stunted trees and brush for the desired width and length for the airfield, she'd take the boys up there with her after school, and weekends to clear brush, rocks and stumps. Both boys remember their mother would not take an excuse when they preferred to play elsewhere or go someplace with their friends.

This long range planning paid off and they built their comfortable home on the hill with the airfield close - two, and sometimes three, Super Cubs parked or flying on or off from it. Daphne handled the realtor selling of the land at Gakona, selling five acre plots, the house and 'Bubble Room,' along with the RV parking lot that had been added later. Once an idea entered her head that was feasible, or within reach, it got done even if she had to do it herself. Her daughter Sally remembered her getting tired of asking Cleo to build a porch on their house at Gakona. As with all busy pilots, his flying took priority. So she built it and did almost a professional job. Being a smart wife, she did it when he was tied up with hunters and the porch was finished when he came home. She had had a little practice at carpentry work at Meiers when they were building and adding on. If some project got started, but not finished, she would get impatient and finish it herself.

Being a bush pilot's wife there wasn't much of anything she couldn't do if she set her mind to it. Cooking for hunters during the seasons wasn't one of her talents, or favorite activities, but she cooked a good meal if it had to be done. When at Meiers, Cleo's mother ran a cafe, Maude's Kitchen, and the hunters ate their meals there. Cleo's mother and stepfather started the cafe about 1960, after Meir's Lodge burned down. Maude was a dedicated grandma for the kids and that let Daphne free to do important trips to Anchorage for case groceries, pick up and deliver clients, as well as all the aircraft and machinery parts that had to be gathered up around town. But there was one thing she never overcame. She was afraid to fly, even with a pilot as skilled and experienced as her husband.

The year Cleo bought the new Super Cub he talked her into flying over to Tanada Lake to visit the Conkles. He had flown the Cub back to Meiers from Fairbanks and it had low engine time. It was a perfect day (weather wise and no pressing needs), to go pleasure flying. All was beautiful until nearing the Copper River a loud bang in the engine got the pilot's attention real fast! He was too busy looking for a place to land on the Copper River to think about Daphne in the seat behind him. He had never said anything about what it might be. He simply turned and said he was going to land in the river and taxi to the bank. Her knuckles were already white from the hand holds on the metal framing. She hadn't seen any sign of houses or people within miles of where they were at. Cleo noticed the plane wasn't losing altitude, so before leaving sight of the river, he turned and said they could make it on to Tanada Lake. "If it's closer to home lets go home!" She yelled back.

After the plane landed on Tanada Lake, without any further scares, Bud had a spark plug he could give Cleo and they tightened the other plugs, and went over the engine carefully, then assured Daphne it was safe to fly home. The loud noise in the cowling was a spark plug that had loosened and blown out.

As long a period as the McMahans and Conkles had been

friends over the years this was Daphne's first trip to Tanada Lake. Her and LeNora enjoyed the afternoon until it came time for them to fly back home. "Oh, my poor babies At home, what if something happens to me? I wish there was some way I could go home on the highway!" she said, but at Tanada lake it was; "fly out only or walk." She might have walked if Cleo hadn't convinced her she'd be home in an hour. If she elected to walk, it could be two days!

While driving the school bus, or at home, Daphne was the disciplinarian and always managed to handle the situations before they got out of hand. Her son Chuck remembers the few times she would stop the bus and walk back to the rear of the bus to stop a fight, or discipline a trouble maker. The kids on the bus respected her and seldom gave her trouble.

Chuck laughs every time he thinks about the time he and Harley talked back to her and when she took after them they climbed the nearby handy tree. She came out of the house carrying the 22 rifle. They both practically fell out of the tree thinking she was going to shoot the limbs off. It didn't take long to be on the ground in time to see her shoot a chattering squirrel in the next tree that had been chewing up things on the porch. All three had a good laugh that time.

It is very few mothers that don't tolerate the pets kids seem to accumulate, beside the dogs and cats. One of the pets both Harley and Chuck had for a few years, was a Parka squirrel that lived under the house at Gakona, and went with the boys to Meiers. One afternoon LeNora and Colin stopped for a visit and wanting to show Colin the squirrel, she whistled for it. It came running out from under the house and discovering she had no feed for it, it bit her big toe and ran back under the house. Back in the house while bandaging her bleeding toe, she wondered what that rodent had against women. It had never bitten her before, but now would bite any female that came within biting distance. Chuck had a baby caribou calf that its mother had abandoned it. He had been flying with his dad when they spotted it. Then three-hours later they flew back to check and it was obvious mama had abandoned it. It was alone so they brought it home. Chuck was now its mama. When Chuck was in school, it was up to Daphne to hold its bottle of milk. Before going to bed she made sure the calf wasn't in the house with Chuck. At times she'd find him out side sleeping with the calf. It knew where Chuck's bed room was, and would stand under his window making the funny noises caribou calves make when calling momma. Chuck would then spend the rest of the night with it. Cleo wasn't above having pets either — six pet geese! They were something she wasn't fond of. Besides their honking noise, and chasing her, they all spent time on the porch waiting for him to come out, or come home if he was away. Daphne didn't like the slippery mess they covered the porch with. The longer he was away the thicker, and more squirts to step in, over, or scrub off. Daphne kept her kitchen knives sharp, but all those geese survived the dinner table.

At Meiers they had a small generator for electricity, with a bad battery charging capabilities and the battery would run down if the plant was operated too long. Then Coleman lanterns became the source of lights. A few times Daphne cooked dinner for the hunters and if they were chatting in the living room Cleo might excuse himself and head for bed after a long day of flying. Before he went to bed however, he would go out to the shed and shut the light plant down. That left her to light the lanterns and answer the barrage of questions, and carry on a conversation until they left for their own cabin. She didn't hunt, so didn't talk their language, but was adept at keeping the conversations going, while hoping they too would soon leave for bed. It was just another talent she had developed and as a business partner, it made the clients feel comfortable while sharing their home and family.

It wasn't encouraged for a wife to come along with her husband and stay in a base camp. A client; whose name has long since been forgotten, was an exception. This couple had a camper and wanted to park it in there yard at Meiers if Cleo should take him sheep hunting. It just happened that he had an assistant guide that was free on that first hunt. Before he made the hunt with the McMahan Guide and Flying Service, the man told them he had a heart condition but kept himself in good physical condition.

"I know my limits and I don't want you to feel uncomfortable about taking me on this hunt or to feel obligated to any special service. I'd prefer to die on a mountain in Alaska's great outdoors doing what I love to do in preference to a lingering death in a hospital bed. Making a Dall sheep hunt in Alaska has been my dream, and this could well be my last chance," was the statement he had made.

He died of a heart attack in their camp within a few days of his arrival in hunting camp, and one day after a climb in the sheep hills. These were traumatic times for all concerned - the business, the family, as well as the wife, with only Daphne to console her. It was not only an upsetting time in schedules but getting the State Troopers, and the coroner, in to the isolated hunting camp. One has to have a sympathetic nature in dealing with situations like this, as well as being able to be the important 'go-between' for the variety of traffic still coming through.

Daphne's daughter, Sally's Comments:

My mother is petite, polite, always considerate of others, and always busy. Anyone dealing with her in business found her to be fair, but a tough lady to deal with if they thought she was a pushover, or uninformed. She knew what the facts were. When she wrote up the contract for the high school bus run. She had the figures for the mileage, the fuel consumption, and what her commission would be. Her bid was accepted.

She bought and sold real estate with a fair profit, did the income tax for their own business as well as for other local business, drove the kids to their basket ball and athletic games they were involved with (until we had a license to drive ourselves). I remember her being on the PTA and some other community office. I don't remember ever hearing my mother complain about lack of modern conveniences all those years we lived at Meiers. She accepted the frontier life when she married my father. If something wasn't right she did something to correct it. She set a good example for her children.

After all the years of safe driving in Alaska, with icy winter roads, and varieties of hazardous conditions, it was ironic that her only automobile accident was on the Gakona hill (spoken of earlier), which almost cost her life. The hill was icy and a woman driver lost control of her car on that ice, slammed into Daphne's car, not once but twice! It was in a situation where Daphne had no way of avoiding the approaching, out of con-

trol car. *Apparently the other driver applied brakes on glare ice. It was several days, while Daphne remained in intensive care (in the Anchorage Hospital), before the family knew she would survive. Only with God's blessing, is she is still with us.*

Daphne's son, Chuck's comments:

My mother was a bush pilot's wife but that wasn't all. She was a devoted mother, a secretary for some of the local organizations, school bus driver, good cook and housekeeper, carpenter and business woman. She was a loving wife (of forty-six-years as of now), a homesteader, a surveyor and an ambitious lady. She was her own architect and drew detailed house plans of future houses. She played piano at Church and was not only a faithful attendant but saw to it that all four of us kids attended with her. By the example she set, was responsible for all four of us kids to grow up with a strong Christian Faith.

Age, and the bad car accident, has now gotten to her body and mind, but when she does leave us I'll remember my mom as a strong, determined woman, who worked for what she got and could do anything she put her mind to.

Chapter Twelve

Evelyn Bunch

In the summer of 1959, the year Alaska officially became a state, Evie Bly, (as she was known then) decided to fly to Alaska from her native state of New York in search of adventure and to finish her college education at the University Of Alaska in Fairbanks. She was 23 years old and single at the time she arrived. She had less than $100 in her pocket but she had no doubt she could find work until college started in the fall.

Three days after arriving in Fairbanks she was hired as a cocktail waitress at the Traveler's Inn. While working there she met a young man by the name of Ken Bunch but she did not meet him again until almost a year later. One evening he arrived at the apartment she shared with two roommates. He had a date with the girl who was a stewardess and she introduced Ken to Evie. Not long after this meeting, the stewardess was transferred to Seattle and Ken called Evie to ask her out on a date. She accepted and that was the beginning of a year long courtship. Evie had learned that Ken was a high school teacher and part-time commercial pilot. He had been a pilot since a teenager in Oklahoma and came to Alaska to fulfill his dream of flying in Alaska and eventually to have his own flying service. He was only 30 years old but he was determined to make it happen some day.

In the spring of 1961 Evelyn graduated from UAF with a Bachelor's Degree in Education. While she was home in New York for the summer, Ken convinced her to return to Alaska and marry him that fall. As a teaching couple they moved to Old Harbor on Kodiak Island the next year was by design, dedicated to gaining experience teaching and living in the bush. As life in the bush can be, and usually is, harsh. It demands attention to detail. In time they saved enough money to purchase their first aircraft, a Cessna 170 on floats, and Ken flew it across the treacherous waters between the mainland and Kodiak Island. They enjoyed the somewhat isolated bush life of living in a small community. There were no roads here and no telephones. Everything and everybody arrived by airplane or boat.

One stormy day in May of 1963 Evelyn was transported by air to the hospital in Kodiak to give birth to their first daughter, Bebe.

That summer Ken had been hired by HARVEY'S FLYING SERVICE to fly salmon fry from a hatchery to various lakes on the Island. It was a lonely time for Evelyn as she stayed behind and cared for the new baby. By fall they had accepted a new teaching assignment at Gakona, Alaska, about 200 miles north of Anchorage. This was another small community with a two-teacher school, but this was on the highway system with an airstrip in front of the school. Ken could view his airplane, now on wheels, from his classroom windows.

Although teaching had its rewards and appeals, Ken yearned to be a pilot full time, so, soon after arriving in Gakona he applied for and received authorization to operate a flying service under the Department of Transportation in Alaska. They named their business SPORTSMAN FLYING SERVICE. He flew his own clients, mainly fish and game biologists, hunters, and fishermen in the summer months for the next three years. Evelyn assisted in a variety of ways from home.

In March of 1966 a second daughter, Holly, was born. That spring Ken made the decision to retire from teaching and begin a full time business of flying and guiding big game hunters.

Ken and Evelyn would no longer be a teaching couple so they left Gakona to homestead on 160 acres of land they had acquired in 1965. Now they lived 20 miles south west of Glennallen on a lake big enough to operate a floatplane. Evelyn continued to teach elementary school children, now in the Glennallen school, while Ken began a busy flying service, catering to nonresidents hunters he would fly into wilderness camps for big game trophies. As guiding and outfitting hunters became a bigger part of his business, Ken was frequently away from home during Alaska's hunting seasons.

As their business picked up Evelyn became more involved not only in the summer months but after school hours as well. She spent many hours expediting equipment and hunting supplies, answering hunters questions, writing letters to prospective clients and doing the bookkeeping. Even the girls, as they were growing older, pitched in to help. Bebe, being the older daughter was soon pumping water out of the pontoons, running errands, and fueling the floatplane. Holly followed and proved to be a big help in the business too. The many times Evelyn would drive to Anchorage to meet their nonresident hunters and bring them back—a six hour round trip. The two girls were put in charge of cleaning the lodge and getting things ready for the hunters arrival.

In the early 1960s until 1970, many of the Alaska pilots were going to Barrow and Kotzebue for the polar bear hunts which were growing in popularity. Clients from the Lower 48 were plentiful and eager to make that hunt. They had the money to pay the going price. Considering the distance those pilots flew from their home bases, length of the hunts as well as delays due to weather, they could be gone from home as long as two months. Ken and his flying partner— this was called the buddy-system—where one pilot flies watch, and/or, additional gear for the polar bear hunts out from Kotzebue. Those hunts were conducted in February and March. Evelyn, Ken's partner at home, was the business manager at their hanger located at the Gulkana Airport, as well as getting the girls off to school and keeping things going at home, paying the bills, booking clients for the fall hunts and handling the emergencies that always seemed to happen as soon as Ken was out of reach. She always managed and any problem was taken care of by the time he returned.

Ken was gone for long periods of time during the fall hunts in the Wrangell Mountains, brown bear on the Alaska Peninsula and coastal areas. He aerial wolf hunted during the winter months. Seldom was there means of communication when the pilots, doing this type of flying, were away from home. The wife at home with the kids and many responsibilities, grew accustomed to listening for the sound of their returning airplane and a husband home safe again after another eventful hunt.

Evelyn loved to fly with Ken and went flying with him every opportunity that presented itself. He was a "born-pilot" and she always felt safe flying anywhere with him, or when one or the

Evelyn fleshing a caribou hide.

other of the girls was in the airplane with him. She never had a chance to go aerial wolf hunting with him but knew she would have enjoyed giving that a try. Very few of the pilots and guides had time to take their wives hunting or flying with them. Ken was always busy and Evelyn was obligated at home but she managed to take ground school and then flying lessons in a Super Cub on skis. She didn't get her private pilot's license but Ken would let her handle the controls of their airplane wherever they were flying to add to her confidence, she knew she could fly it, land or take off, if she ever had to.

Her life was busy when she was teaching school but she made time to be a guide pilot's wife on weekends and when school was out for the summer. Winter months she helped with the skinning and fleshing of the animals Ken trapped and then some of the big game animals shot by their clients in preparation for transporting to the Taxidermist. Very few wives could be persuaded to add that meticulous task to there busy schedule. She not only was willing, but prided herself on doing a professional job of it.

There was an occasional hunt in the mountains for sheep and moose when they had no hunters. But Evelyn could hunt right from the front porch of their log home on Tolsona Lake near Glennallen. She shot her first moose right from the porch that looked out toward the lake. It was all butchered, cut up, packaged and in the freezer when Ken returned from his hunt empty handed. She is so small it makes one ask, "did she handle that big animal alone or call on some one to help?" It wouldn't be too surprising to me to know she did it alone.

When they started outfitting with horses, as many as thirteen at one time, there had to be many stories. Neither Ken nor Evelyn had ever worked with horses or been around them much and anyone familiar with horses know that horses sense that and take advantage. Even an old experienced "Dude" horse will do things it wouldn't try with an experienced rider on its back. A favorite trick is to sidle nonchalantly alongside the trail to a low branch and brush the rider off, or it may sense the rider on its back is sleeping if the reins are loose. This is the ideal time to jump over a fallen log instead of stepping over it. NOTE: I'll let Evelyn tell in her own words, one of their experiences when outfitting with horses: Dealing with horses was a lot of trial and error with Ken and me because neither one of us had much experience with them as pack animals or had to care for them on a yearly basis. Most of our experience had been pleasure riding, as youngsters, on the farm. When we made the decision to offer guided hunts on horse back, about 1969, we started shopping for horses in places like Palmer and Delta Junction. Even there we didn't have many to choose from. The first two we bought were a half broke mare we planned to use as a pack horse and an older gelding who was better trained but wasn't entirely gentle. He was named Gray Legs and had a reputation for being hard to handle.

We had those two horses only a short time when, under the care of a hired hand, they got loose while we were away on a weekend. When we returned home Ken looked for them by air off and on all summer but could not locate them. Then in late fall, when the lakes were frozen over, another pilot spotted the two runaways on a lake many miles to the south of Tolsona lake where there are no roads, only stunted black spruce, and seismic trails. We were elated and made plans to get our horses home. Ken's idea was to fly me out in our Super Cub along with grain and riding tack. He figured if the horses weren't too wild after being on their own all summer maybe we could coax them to us with grain, then gradually test Gray Legs to see if he'd accept the bridal and saddle. Of course my part in this plan was to ride this "wild" gelding back to Tolsona Lake and hope the mare would follow. We figured this to be about a 12 mile ride.

We landed some distance from the horses and shaking the grain in a bucket slowly approached them. They shied away at first but were enticed closer by the oats rattling in the bucket. They both came cautiously and with his nose in the bucket slurping oats, Gray Legs didn't flinch when Ken put a rope around his neck, then a bridle and with much patience and talking to him in a soothing voice, put the saddle on his back. Ken let the horse get used to it before he cinched it tight and put some weight on it. Gray Legs didn't buck or rear so we assumed he was rideable. Now it was my turn to get aboard. I admit I was nervous about what could happen but actually welcomed the challenge. I mounted and let the horse get used to me in the saddle while Ken held onto the bridle, talking and petting the horse. Gray Legs danced around a bit but accepted our authority. Ken assured me he would be watching from the air to be sure I was okay all the way. Before Ken taxied the Cub and was airborne, I was headed south on a seismic trail with the mare following. I was still somewhat nervous and singing aloud to calm myself and the horses. As we crossed from one trail to the next, keeping in the right direction, we occasionally came across a flock of ptarmigan that would flutter up in the air ahead of us. This would excite Gray Legs, dancing and backing up while I held the reins tight and talking to him he'd relax again.

Ken had landed and was home when I reached the north shore of Tolsona Lake with my two charges. I decided to go across the lake because it was the shortest way. Once we were out on the frozen lake the ice started cracking and groaning. Gray Legs didn't want any part of this. He balked, pranced sideways, backward and wanted to be someplace else. So did I. We were back on the shore as quickly as his legs would take us. We followed the shore and then up the airstrip. The corral was close. Just as we were in sight, Ken let the other horses out onto the air field thinking these horses would be happy to join them. We had purchased these other horses and brought them home after Gray Legs and the mare had left. These horses didn't want strangers joining them and ran at us, teeth bared, bucking and heels kicking up there heals. Gray Legs was kicking and jumping while I was trying to keep my feet in the stirrups and protect my legs from getting assaulted, all the while screaming at my husband. We had a "rodeo" until Ken figured out how to get the loose horses back in the corral. I survived without a scratch, still aboard my bucking bronco, but I was furious with Ken who had only good intentions. (Trial and errors with an okay ending.)

Those fist two years that we used pack and saddle horses, our hired wranglers had to ride and lead them a distance of eighty miles deep into the Wrangell mountains to our hunting camp at Big Bend Lakes MaCCall Ridge. Before their long ride began, we trucked the horses from the homestead on Tolsona Lake to Chitna where they had to swim the swift flowing Copper River. On the opposite shore was the beginning of the old "sixty one mile" railroad bed leading to McCarthy. (Now there is a long modern bridge at this site). Crossing the Copper River was perilously risky. To swim the horses across it was imperative to wait for the water level and all conditions to be right. We hired a trustworthy local man with a boat and powerful, dependable motor to help the boys get the horses to the opposite side. The most experienced wrangler would sit in the back of the boat holding a length of rope to the halter of a horse that would swim and drift diagonally downriver to the opposite shore. Once on shore it was tied to a tree and then return across the river to get another one until all the horses were safely across. This was a nerve wracking procedure. No one relaxed until "mission accomplished."

'Murphy's Law' was always in force no matter how carefully we all planned and worked. A couple of times a horse pulled away from the wrangler and tried to swim on its own. At times a horse would get caught in the swift current, and with its head under water, become disorientated, while tumbling over, and over, first its hooves surfacing, the next moment its head would pop up. The first time I saw this happen I was sure the horse was a "goner" and would end up in Cordova downriver. Luckily we never lost a horse. Sometimes a horse got loose and had to be rounded up causing long delays.

I was never able to go along on these trips but I did witness the crossings at Chitna River and Ken related any unusual happenings on his return. The second year all the men went with the horses, so I had to drive the truck and horse trailer home. I was given a quick check-ride and sent on my way. My heart was pounding. I wasn't sure I was cut out for this job but there was no one else to do it. With each mile my confidence improved and by the time I was halfway home I was feeling like a real trucker.

There were a few times business required a second pilot when Ken was involved with getting the horses to camp before the hunters were due to arrive. He had the flying to do while supervising the wranglers in the various stages of progress. Ken hired the guides and wranglers, supplied the camps, supervised the hunts and gave all the orders. In the early days before they used horses he did many of the backpack hunts himself. There were times he flew to Anchorage to fly their hunting clients out to camp or return them after the hunt.

Our first three years with the horses we would bring them out after the fall hunting season and boarded them in Palmer over the winter months. This was an ordeal for men and horses. Later we found out those earlier big game outfitters who used horses kept them on the Chitna River bar all winter and they thrived on the abundance of pea-vine growing there. We applied to the BLM for a grazing lease near Bryson Bar, where we had another hunting camp and Ken could fly there to keep track of them and feed them grain if necessary. That turned out to be practical.

The emergencies the girls and I had while Ken was away predominantly involved snow and cold weather. One early spring when Ken was at Kotzebue on polar bear hunts it snowed heavily overnight and was still snowing in the morning. We worried about forcing the old station wagon through deep snow on the mile of our homestead road to the highway. This was a school day and we needed to be there. By flooring the gas pedal and the three of us holding on for dear life as the station wagon bounced over ruts and slithered from one side of the road to the other, we made it to the highway, there it quit! Opening the hood, I found the engine encased in snow. All three of us worked with our mittened hands to scoop the snow out then try starting it. It started, but there were other times in deep snow it would not start right away, and usually not at all. Our only option then was to hitchhike the twenty miles from Tolsona Lake to Glennallen. We were late for school more than once.

In those early years we didn't have a garage to keep the car warm overnight. During severe cold spells we used to plug in the headbolt heater but there were still times the car refused to start. We'd bundle up and head down the road on foot to hitchhike once more. There wasn't much traffic on the roads in those years but we'd always get a ride, nearly always with the first car that came along. Once a kindly trucker, driving a 10-wheeler, stopped for us. He set the girls up in the sleeper section and me in the passenger seat and off we went. The girls loved the ride.

There were grizzly bears in the woods where we had our homestead and occasionally a black bear. We have had bear get into our hunting camps but never here at the cabin. Some came in our yard and it worried me when the girls were playing out of my sight.

A very big grizzly was fishing by the dock one day when Ken was returning with two clients back from a hunt. Taxiing across the lake he sighted the bear before he floated the plane alongside the dock. To frighten it away he reeved up the plane's engine and made circles in front of the dock until the bear reluctantly decided to fish elsewhere.

"Evelyn, where are the girls?" was my husband's concern as

he took notice of the direction the bear was heading. He knew they could be playing somewhere in the vicinity. Luckily they were close to the house and I was warned to keep a lookout for that grizzly. It might return if it thought fish still available.

Sometime later the girls and I were driving down our road, rounded a curve and encountered a large blond grizzly sitting in the middle of the road with its back to us. I stopped the car to see what it was going to do. It sat awhile before realizing we were there. He looked over his shoulder, got up and loped quite a distance down the road ahead of us and finally went into the bushes along side the road. We never saw that one again and was sure it was a different bear than the one Ken saw fishing at the dock. This one was a lighter color hue than the one Ken described. Just seeing one this close to home keeps one on the alert.

Ken was home the time a large grizzly visited us a couple of times in the middle of the night. The first time it swatted the side of the house where our bedroom was and woke us up. The sound was like a wrecking ball hitting the outer wall. Ken jumped out of bed to see what the noise was all about. He parted the curtain and saw the grizzly coming around the corner of the house.

"You want to see a real big grizzly bear? Come look!" Ken said.

Being curious and protected, I peeked out and we were face to face with that bear. It was looking in and we were looking out. Ken waved his arms and let out a loud "Shoooo-ha—ha—ha." It jumped back, raised up on its hind legs to look again then bounded off into the woods.

The second time that same bear came back there was something in our pickup truck it liked the smell of. We heard it during the night and looked out. It was embracing the camper shell on the truck. Ken waved his arms and let out his loud screeching, bear scaring yell! The bear dropped down on all fours and ran for the woods. It was the last we saw of that one and I was always in hopes that if that one, or any others came around I would prefer they came while Ken was home.

Another time an inquisitive bear would pass by the house on a regular basis, stand on its hind legs and swipe its front paws across our bedroom window. It never broke the glass, maybe because the window was thermopane, and it never attempted to break in the door or destroyed anything around the place. Its paw prints were unmistakable and were left frequently

In 1978 SPORTSMAN FLYING SERVICE started operating at the Gulkana Airport where we had a hanger built and we continued to operate the floatplane base at Tolsona Lake. With the wheel-plane base at Gulkana - GULKANA AIR SERVICE was added to our FAA certificate. I was still teaching school and the girls were growing. As the business grew we bought a Super Cub, then traded the 170B for a Cessna 180, then traded that for a Cessna 185 on floats. From this point the business grew to include a Cessna 206 and eventually a 207 and various other aircraft. Now the business required more pilots than just Ken, who had been doing the majority of the flying. Ken went all the way to St Louis, Missouri to buy his Super Widgeon and received his multi-engine rating in Seattle on his way home. He was proud of his Widgeon N101KB. It was his "Signature" aircraft and he had quite a few adventures and near incidents while flying it. The Widgeon was a good work horse for hauling hunters and freight.

The many times when Ken was overdue, I would convince myself he was detained due to weather. Then the time he was long overdue because of weather conditions, it turned out to be more than an incident.

It was the day Ken didn't return from a flight to pick up two Japanese mountain climbers in the Wrangell Mountains. Evelyn was at the hanger that morning and helped him push the ski equipped Cessna 185 out of the Gulkana hanger. It was the first clear morning after many days of clouds and snow. The day was April 16, 1991. Ken was anxious to get going before the weather turned bad again. This flight to the Nabesna glacier would take no more than two hours, he calculated. He marked the place on the map where he would be landing. It was at the 8000 foot elevation near Mt. Jarvis, which the climbers planned to scale. Everything looked good for a normal glacier landing. After Ken flew off for the pick up, she waited in the hanger for his return. Two hours went by with no radio call from Ken. No messages to let her know where he was or why he couldn't return. The radio he had in his airplane could reach the Flight Station and in accordance with procedures, had filed a flight plan. Her worry now was starting turn to fear.

Then the FAA (Federal Aviation Administration) Flight Service Station called her to say Ken was overdue on his flight plan and if he didn't return within the half hour they would send the local Civil Air Patrol out to search for him. She prayed that he would return in that half hour — but he did not. Several local CAP pilots took to the air to search the area of his intended landing. By this time the weather had closed in, and none of the pilots could fly even close to that high elevation in the mountains. The CAP called off the search as darkness arrived. Meanwhile Evelyn was trying to keep her mind on other things to control her fear that something

Ken Bunch high in the mountains with his Super Cub.

had happened to the airplane on landing or the weather had closed in on him while he was loading the two men and their gear and simply couldn't see to take off. She knew he would be upset about having to stay overnight with minimal camping gear on the cold glacier ice. The two Japanese climbers would just have to share their tent and camping equipment. She comforted herself that he would use good judgment and not fly in the mountains if he had no visuals. But how long would it be before the weather improved? He was simply waiting for the weather to clear, but deep down she couldn't help but wonder if something serious had happened—a broken ski on landing or …. There were so many possibilities and unknowns. People started calling to express their concerns. Evelyn tried to assure them everything would be okay.

The next day the FAA had contacted the Air National Guard and asked them to assist in the search. Weather continued to be stormy in the mountains. Finally by 4:30 PM on the second day the National Guard in reaching Ken and the two climbers. They radioed to the FAA that they had three souls aboard (meaning they were carrying three passengers.) Receiving this message, Evelyn was relieved and elated. Sounded like everybody was okay and just a problem with the aircraft. No details had been given in the communication to the FAA.

When the National Guard Helicopter landed by the Park Service hanger, two State Trooper cars met the helicopter. Evelyn watched as they passed by her hanger. She wondered why Ken and the others did not come in to their hanger. Soon a pilot friend, Dwayne King, stopped in to see Evelyn and volunteered to see what was going on. A short time later he returned and he looked very serious and said he had good news and some bad. These are the words he used; "First the good news. The airplane was fine. Ken did not have an accident. The plane was exactly where Ken intended to land to pick up the climbers. The bad news…." She could hear her heart beat faster and readied herself. She had no inkling of how bad the news was going to be. "Ken didn't make it!" King simply stated.

Her first thoughts were, "what could he mean? Surely he did not die!" He was only days away from being 62 years old and reasonably healthy, he seemed fine the day he left, not ill, or tired, just his normal self. So what happened? As Dwayne went on to relay the information he had found out; Ken had died of a sudden heart attack! To say this was a shock to her, as well as to family and friends, was an understatement !!!

Details of the event on the mountain were translated by a local Japanese lad who talked to the climbers. They didn't speak English and they didn't know how to operate the radio in the airplane. They had all exerted themselves trying to manually turn the airplane around in the heavy fresh snow, so Ken could take off in the proper direction. Then they tried to taxi and get up speed for take off, but discovered they needed to lighten the climbers gear. Ken stopped to unload some of the gear and in the process stepped away from the plane and collapsed in the snow! The climbers tried to revive him but failed. A later autopsy revealed that Ken had a heart condition, which under stress and high elevation, probably caused his demise.

Evelyn had retired from teaching earlier, and at the time, was working with Ken at their hanger. She continued to operate the business for a short time and then sold the flying service. She retired to a quiet life at her lovely log home on Tolsona Lake.

The Girls were with her and helped her adjust. Both girls had soloed — Bebe on her 16th birthday, Holly while in college, and both girls did some "cross country time." Eventually both girls went on to do there own thing.

Input by Evelyn's daughter Bebe

As an adult I have come to realized who my mother really is. I know that she was raised on a farm in New York. She worked on that farm, cared for her younger brother, sisters and took care of the household. As a teen she worked to put herself through college but before she finished she left for Alaska for the adventure and finished her college education at he University of Alaska then obtained her Masters in Education. Among other things I found out about my mother—she has been a model, Miss Alaska in the Miss Universe Pageant, flight attendant, teacher in the bush schools, and handled the business end of the family guide and air taxi business. She is a wonderful artist although she refuses to recognize this. My mom skis, skates, runs marathons, roller blades, and keeps an enviable figure. One would think "Wow, what a gal," but as a child I thought all moms did these things. As I grew older I realized this was not the case. I have watched my mom go from peeling logs while we were building our house, answering business inquires to skinning animals, taking art classes, cooking dinner, making sure my sister and I were ready for school or ballet class, plus working full time on a teaching job.

Every day living on the homestead wasn't always easy for her either. After we moved to the homestead at Tolsona from Gakona, we lived in a two-bedroom trailer house. Since we didn't have a well, twice a week mom would haul water home from the public water source twenty miles from us in Glennallen. Water was precious and not wasted. (It wasn't until I was in college that a well and washing machine and dryer was in service at home. Later as the business grew, my parents built a lovely home near the lake. During the construction transition we were able to upgrade from an out-house to indoor plumbing. The gravity feed water storage system wasn't without flaws however. The storage tank in our attic was larger than our previous water drum, but had more use, so water had to be hauled more frequently. If there were delays in driving from Glennallen in the deep winter cold, the water would start to freeze. Eventually my dad built our own "Trans Alaska Pipeline" It was for water to be pumped out of the lake to the house storage tank in the attic. It was a relief for my mom not to have to haul water on the back of the pickup truck anymore. Although the pipeline was heat-taped, it sometimes froze. I remember many a time my mother boiling water and pouring it down the 1 inch hose in the attic to thaw the pipeline. Next she would hook up the vacuum cleaner exhaust to force the hot water to the ice plug. (I'm not sure which of my parents figured this solu-tion to a frozen hose). She'd then run to the porch and yell down to the lake to ask Ken if he saw any signs of thawing yet? This ritual could go on for hours and a feeling of accom-plishment when we could hear the water gurgling into the storage tank pumped from the hole drilled through the ice on the lake. Mom's old nylons tied over the end of the hose completed our filtration system.

Frozen water also presented a problem on the road to our house in the winter months. After the battles of building a mile long road from the highway, across and around swampy areas, to our house on the lake, a massive glacier formed over it from the hot springs in the swamp, making the road impassable until spring. For a few winters we would all would park across the lake at our office-aircraft hanger and then walk or snowma-chine the half mile across between home and the car. I can well remember the time when my dad was away on the hunts, the car broke down and stranded all three of us on the highway, we stood there for a long time (on a deep cold winter day waiting for a ride.) The truck that stopped to give us a ride took us all the way to the school house - an 18-wheeler and I was so impressed I decided I was going to be a truck driver.

"Are you sure there's nothing else you'd rather be?" Mother asked. After thinking it over I decided maybe I'd rather ride in a rodeo. Much to mother's relief, I did neither.

My sister and I had an assortment of animals—all our very own pets—a horse, cat, dog and chickens. At the time there wasn't a veterinarian anywhere around so mom would drive to the hospital in Glennallen to get medicine for my horse, or the dog with a face full of porcupine quills, not to mention the 30 some horses we had later in the hunting business. To this day I tease my sister that our horses and dogs had the same doctor that delivered her. During those early years those first two doctors at Faith Hospital kept a file on all the horses and dogs that were always being brought in for cuts, porcupine quills or worms.

When I was about 12 years old (the age when girls start being obnoxious, self- centered and having an attitude). Mom sent me to look for my horse Pony, because she hadn't been seen for a day and she never missed a meal. Thinking she was overreacting, I set out to look but was mad because I was going to a school doings that evening and wanted to curl my hair and get ready. I reluctantly went to look but came back without finding it. Mom said we are going to find Pony before you go anywhere. We looked for twenty minutes or more and I huffed back to sit in the car not sure if I was mad at Pony or mom. In a few minutes I saw mom leading my horse. Pony was limping badly and bleeding. She had been caught in barbed wire from an abandoned corral, panicked trying to get free and cutting her legs badly. I was mortified and so ashamed of my actions. If it hadn't been for Mom, Pony would have been a barbed wire pot roast for a bear or wolves. That was a lesson mother taught me about priorities and persistence by example rather than punishment or scolding.

Other valuable lessons I learned were often because Mom allowed Holly and I freedom for creativity and testing of boundaries. We built forts in the woods, captured rabbits and learned that fire can creep to a Joy soap bottle faster than you can squeeze the gas out of it. We poked at the intestines of skinned wolves, found out that if you ride a horse backwards you will be bucked off and above all, it's best not to push your sister off the roof of an aircraft hanger with an army parachute (the test run with a tire - the chute never opened). The earliest lesson I remember is when I was about 4 years old. I wanted to build a sand castle. I didn't have the standard sand bucket and shovel, but Mom made do and sent me out with Tupperware and the "Big Tony" spoon. Don't ask me where the spoon got that name. I just know it was large, used for mixing cookies and spanking—and it was metal. When mama says don't lick the "Tony Spoon" when it's 5 degrees below zero, it's best not to, or you'll be running to mama with a bloody tongue.

Years later I was able to use this knowledge on the kids from Texas who migrated to Glennallen during the Alyeska Pipeline construction days. Metal swings and spoons have a lot in common. There was more I could teach these Dudes who came from the Lower 48 from a warmer climate, who I often came in contact with because I also was working for the pipeline and hadn't made a career of a truck driver, or in a rodeo. Everyday living on a homestead wasn't always easy for mother. There were difficult days, but we had many that were exciting and fun. The nature of a family business probably allowed us to spend more time together than more conventional families. We shared the excitement and work of the many hunters who came and went during the fall hunting seasons. Horses and supplies gathered for hunting camps. The evenings might find us sitting on the floor in the living room by the Fifty-five-gallon drum barrel stove fleshing and salting sheep hides. There were always aircraft, tents, packs and saddles to get ready. Lifting airplanes on home built tripods by the lake to change from floats to skis in the spring and fall was always a family affair.

Even with the hectic schedule of the air taxi business and teaching, Mom would make time to do thoughtful things for Holly and me. I especially remember the matching red dresses Mom sewed for us. I thought we were so elegant in them. Dad was proud of the red wing covers she made for the airplane. Holly and I were excited with the baby chicks she brought home for us one Easter. She let us keep them in a box in our bedroom until we were convinced no one can sleep with a dozen chicks peeping all night. When the chicks grew bigger Holly and I helped Mom build a chicken coop out of scrap lumber from around the homestead. She showed us how to take what seemed like nothing and create something of value. Eventually my horse broke down the chicken wire around their coop to eat the chicken feed. We gave up trying to keep that mischievous horse in her corral. Now the liberated chickens had free range. It now was more difficult to find and collect eggs.

When I was 13 years old my mother came home from Anchorage with a new motorcycle in the back of the pickup truck. I had begged for a year to have a motorcycle instead of an allowance for working at the hanger. I was elated—my father was not. He never worried about my flying but he told my mother that "thing" was going back because I would end up killing myself. Mom defended my need to have a motorcycle. Dad ended up taking his next flight of hunters and when he got back there was 15 miles on the motorcycle (I had never been on one before). Taking the motorcycle back was never discussed again. The thrill and excitement of having that motorcycle, working for it and having my mother standing up for me outweighed the risk of the times I did almost kill myself. Mom had never said to either of her daughters; "You can't do that!...you're a girl, you're to small, it's too dangerous, or you'll get hurt." My mom has an adventurous spirit and recognized my need to learn from experiences but to use good judgment as well.

My childhood in the bush was unique. It was sometimes harsh. I watched my parents work hard and I am strong and capable because of it.

These things I came to know and trust:

It's best not to wash maggots off the animal skulls (that have been setting around) in your swimming area of the lake.

Mom can kill chickens by ringing their necks over her head. (I will not eat a chicken I have kissed on the head).

If you paint the outhouse with flowers, monkeys, lions etc., Mom will say it's beautiful, let's take a picture of it and send it back to Grandpa in New York.

If you can outrun Mom around the dining room table when she is going to spank you, she will eventually start laughing, but best not to get on the top bunk bed when she is after you with the broom.

Don't come back and tell her you can't find it when she sends you after something.

"Find it, fix it, or make one," she will say.

My mom still loved me even after I punched down her dinner rolls before they were ready and she was expecting company for dinner. Put a dent in her car.

Used a piece of her good silverware to roast marshmallows over the burn barrel.

I even knocked her off her feet in the back of the water hauling truck with a 4 inch hose because I accidentally turned it on full instead of off.

My Mom can be painting and have a brown paper bag over her freshly set hair, with a comb to match the black dress she'll be wearing to the party her and Dad will be going to that evening.

She will water-ski when it's snowing, she just needs a down jacket!

Enough of children's memories:

Now Evelyn lives in a private aviation community in Palmer and has all the modern conveniences she wants. She can use her Cellular phone to call the auto club if her German BMW won't start. She will shoot a caribou off the front porch of the old homestead, or like she did last year when she was 60 years old, hunt mountain goat in the Chugach Mountain Range. She enjoys climbing some of the roughest mountain ranges in Alaska, and drying wool socks over a Coleman burner, wet from a glacial rain and windstorm, in a two-man tent with her sweaty daughter and son-in-law. The simple pleasures in life for her is a challenge: her family, and flying home in a Super Cub after a day in the hills with a bucket of blueberries on her lap.

My mother was worthy of the title; she was indeed a real Alaskan, and a true bush pilot's wife.

Evelyn's daughter Holly's input.

I first became aware of who my mother was when she was an elementary teacher in the school at Gakona. After a day at school she'd take my sister and me with her to the air taxi business she and my father operated, and she'd continue to do all the paper work and public relations for the business. Then she'd grade the papers from school late into the night. Bebe and I slept there until she went home unless our dad took us home with him. She was a hard worker but never complained about the hours or the type of work she was doing. She can adjust to any situation she is exposed to. She would serve on various committees in the community, and a class at our Church on Sundays. She was a great people person and well liked in our community and as a teacher. She could even make clients happy when the weather was too bad for my dad to fly them out to their camps or when the flight got behind schedule.

As a child, my mother fascinated me with some of the things she would do. One year after the ice went out on the lake and before wet suits, I watched her water skiing right off the dock, wearing jeans and a down jacket, then coasting onto the beach wet clear above her ankles. I wanted to be able to try that and be as good as she was. Watching her sitting on the floor at the hanger or on the living room floor at home, skinning an animal a hunter shot, would make me wonder if she enjoyed doing it or did it just to help dad with his work. She would let me feel it, pull on the skin and poke at its eyes, and if it was a wolf, feel its big teeth. It was a special occasion for my sister and me if we were allowed to stay up to eat steak when mom cooked a late dinner for some of our clients. It could be as late as 11 PM because the business hours and flights sometimes went later into the night. I think I was the most impressed the time our car stalled on a very cold winter morning when we were on our way to school and my mother hailed a big truck and the driver took us right to the school. It left a real impression on me to ride to school in a semi-truck, but to see my petite little mom hitch hike on the highway so we'd be at school regardless, when we could just as easily gone back home because it was closer.

My sister, our dog and I, used to go bear and moose hunting with our mother. We'd drive away in our old "66 Chevy," or walk. She had her own special lookout tree. She loved to hunt and could take care of the animals she shot.

She has taught me that life is an adventure. Enjoy what you have and always do your best.

Chapter Thirteen

Willy Lou Warbelow

Marvin and Willy Lou met on their first day of college at the Superior State Teachers College in Wisconsin - September 1936. They always kept in touch but lived a hundred-miles apart, so seldom saw one another over the years. They were married in 1945.

1945 they left Wisconsin to come to Alaska and teach in the Eskimo villages of Arctic Alaska: Shungnak, Unalakeet and Selawik. Three years after they were married Marvin had his private pilot's license and a Piper J-5 airplane. He also had big dreams of the type of flying he would do in Alaska. Willy Lou was happy to have a pilot husband and an airplane of their own to feel more comfortable getting a sick baby to a doctor if necessary. The villages where they were teaching, were isolated and dependant on the Bush Pilots from other places. Some were long distances away.

Marvin and Willy Lou in Wisconsin.

They both taught school in the Eskimo villages for eleven years and four children were born to them while they were in the Arctic. The first two, Cyndie and Ron, were born when they were on visits to Wisconsin, and a few years later Art was born in Nome. When Charlie was born they had a Cessna 172 and Marvin flew Willy Lou to Nome for that one and flew them back to Selawik when the baby was two days old. The doctor suggested mother and baby stay longer in the hospital but Marvin knew weather could change and delay them and he was responsible to be back in time for school since he was the only teacher until he and Willy Lou were both back.

Living quarters were rustic in these Eskimo villages but even with four little ones Willy Lou managed. At Selawik and Shungnak their living quarters and class rooms were in the same building. She heard other teachers express a preference for separate buildings so they could get away from the classroom. She liked being able to go back and forth, especially when she had school work to do in the evenings and the kids could play in the class room with her.

With four little ones to care for when Marvin was away flying and too long overdue or missing, were real nightmare for Willy Lou. Especially with lack of communication—no FAA station where he could file a flight plan to keep track of him. He was a loner-type of man with no flying partner so there was no one for him to communicate with and it was up to him to walk back or figure out how to emergency repair his plane and fly it back if he was down some place. There wasn't much Willy Lou could do but worry and wait. Even if he told her where he planned to fly, she had no way to contact him.

There was the time when Marvin had a rough landing on river ice, broke a ski and was back home before she had time to realize he was overdue. Some Eskimos, ice fishing on the river some distance from where he had landed, recognized his plane and saw the rough landing. With their dog teams they went to investigate. They helped him set the broken ski and axle on a sled, hooked up three teams to pull it back up river. They got within a mile of the village, other mushers came out to meet them, tied their teams in front of the already long line of dogs, and arrived on Main street pulling Warbelow's airplane behind thirty-five dogs. What a show for the villagers of Selawik where an airplane was still a novelty.

Eventually Marvin and Willy Lou decided they needed a bigger airplane and since they couldn't afford the new one he was dreaming about, they settled for a Cessna 170 he located via *Trade-A-Plane*. It was in Des Moines, Iowa. They would be visiting their families in Wisconsin when school was out, so with many phone calls and much bartering, it was agreed the plane would be delivered to LaCross, Wisconsin.

When the airplane arrived at the airport and Marvin looked it over carefully, money exchanged, and they both agreed it sure did look big in comparison to their last two. When Marvin made a second trip around the airplane Willy Lou said she could see his expression change from beaming to questioning and becoming more evident with every step. After completing the second circle he turned to her and made this remark, "Lou, I don't think I can fly this airplane!"

"You mean we are heading for the Arctic Circle in Alaska tomorrow morning with two little kids, and you can't fly this airplane?" she gasped.

"I think I'd better get some instructions and make a few landings in it before we leave," he answered after thinking about it awhile and to Willy Lou's sigh of relief.

"How much time have you had in a 170," Marvin asked the instructor he located on short notice and when they were airborne.

"I have never been in a 170 before," the man answered.

Final instructions in the second hand Cessna 170 completed with no casualties, they were on their way home. The two weeks trip from LaCross Wisconsin to Selawik, Alaska was not what Willy Lou described as a pleasure trip with two bored young children confined to the narrow seats, Marvin fighting weather at various times and places, hotels and cafes few and far between, as well as landing fields. This interesting trip is written about in detail in Willy Lou's book; "HEAD WINDS"

1954 the Warbelows had given up their teaching jobs and moved to Cathedral Bluffs on the Alaska Highway. They had submitted the high bid on the old U.S. Army base that was located twenty-five-miles from Tok toward Fairbanks. It eventually became Cathedral Bluffs' Lodge.

They were living at Tetlin where they both had taught at the school for one year, waiting for word that their bid had been accepted for the surplus camp at Cathedral Bluffs. When school was out the spring the family left for Wisconsin and while there, their fourth and last child, Art, was born the same day Marvin left for Waterloo, Iowa to bring back the Cessna 170B he had bought via an ad in *Trade-A-Plane*. He flew the plane back to Alaska, parked it on the airfield at Northway, got a ride back to Wisconsin to bring the family back.

Willy Lou describes this trip back home to Alaska was no easier than the time they flew back in the Cessna 170 but at least it was different. The baby was a month old when they drove a caravan up the Alaska Highway. She drove a 1954 Buick sedan pulling a heavily loaded, two-wheel, trailer. Marvin followed her driving a loaded pickup and towing a small house trailer. At least on this trip all three of the young 'uns didn't have to stay buckled in a seat belt of an airplane all the way. They could ride some times with mama and the baby and then with daddy. Thirteen long muddy days later they crossed the border into Alaska. Then on to Northway where Marvin flew them on to Tetlin in their own airplane, a fifteen minute flight.

Before they could move to their new home they had a major project ahead of them. Cathedral Bluffs installation had been built for the Army by the Alaska Communications System (ACS). It had been used only two years when it was closed and they moved to Tok. The military decided radio reception was too poor there. The communications building was one-hundred-six-feet-long, and twenty- feet wide, good bachelor's quarters, a few smaller buildings and a very nice three-bedroom house that had been the home of the commanding officer. It was within one hundred feet of the Alaska Highway, the Alaska Range right across the road, and the Tanana River in back. It was all boarded up when their bid was accepted and it was still that way when they were starting to move into it.

This would be their own home, the first since they were married, and they had brought back from Wisconsin what they thought they wanted and needed. They hardly had all the boards off the windows and doors, kitchen and bedrooms dusted and liveable, when a construction crew move into the bachelor quarters. Willy Lou cooked two meals a day for them and put up lunches for them each day. Marvin went to work for the bridge construction crew who were rebuilding bridges along the highway. Their evenings and weekends were spent tearing apart and rebuilding the huge communications building, making it into a typical roadhouse like the ones scattered along the Alaska Highway in an earlier day. They soon had a more convenient kitchen organized and they were in the roadhouse business— Cathedral Bluffs Lodge.

A part of the agreement with the construction crew that was boarded there, was that they would bulldoze an airstrip while they were quartered there. They bulldozed out a thousand foot strip beside the highway, reaching from the gas pumps and telephone wires at the upper end to the bridge and the lower end. It was a roughed-out strip that, rightly, wasn't recommend for anyone but a brave and experienced bush pilot to land on. Marvin had his growing boys helping him clear rocks, dig stumps and cut willows every chance he had to be out there. Willy Lou and Cyndie were not excluded from this project when not involved in kitchen tasks that took preference. At long last they had an airfield of their own but the paved highway alongside proved a better landing strip than theirs but the airplane was tied down on their own field.

Alaska bound 1945.

Marvin flew with a private pilot's license until around 1957 then decided he would get a commercial license. There was a big demand for a commercial pilot in the surrounding communities and he had an offer from the Bureau Of Land Management (BLM) to do their flying the next summer. He sold the 170 airplane to Floyd Miller at Northway and again, via *Trade-A-Plane* and another trip to the Lower 48, he flew his next toy (Willy Lou's name for it), a 170B, back home. He spent many hours that winter studying the Jepperson manual and by spring had his commercial pilot's rating.

All four of their growing children were taking correspondence, had been from the beginning of their school years, and a very busy mother was their teacher. They were good students as well as helpful in every capacity, which their mom and dad were involved. All four of them grew up knowing how to fry sourdough pancakes and hamburgers, how to clear tables, wash dishes, run the washing machine, hang up clothes on the outdoor clothes line, make beds and pump gas.

Their lodge at Cathedral Bluffs was a busy place all summer long. Willy Lou had crews of men to cook for: road construction crews, crews that built the towers for the early warning system, surveyors, and a team of geologists who headquartered with them every summer for a few years. Marvin did the flying for the crew of geologists. The construction season was generally over by the fall hunting season and the crews gone. Hunting season was a busier time. They had a bunkhouse that hunters were free to use and Willy Lou nearly always cooked their meals when they came and went. Highway travelers stopped to eat occasionally. Marvin flew fishermen out to outlying lakes and rivers until time to start flying hunters into the hills and mountains. He was now considered to be an Alaskan bush pilot and called upon at all hours of the day and night by a variety of people who wanted to be flown some place.

Marvin now had a floatplane rating and—via *Trade-A-Plane*—a Cessna 170 airplane equipped with pontoons. This plane he bought in Ketchikan and flew it back. He kept it tied down in the Tannana River a short distance in back of the lodge. When the plane wasn't flying some one had to frequently check on it because the water in the river might run low and leave the plane out of the water and it was a project for two helpers to get it afloat again. Or the water could run high, due to melting snow in the hills, and that too created a problem. Now WARBELOW'S AIR VENTURES had a contract to fly the mail and freight from Tok to Tetlin, this besides the flying he was doing for the BLM fire control people.

In the late 1960s they started a weekly flight up the Taylor Highway delivering groceries, repairs for whatever was ordered, to the roadhouses all the way to Eagle and Boundary. Willy Lou would make a trip to Fairbanks every Thursday with the pickup to buy groceries, machinery repairs and whatever had been ordered the week before, plus the shopping for their lodge supplies. That meant a variety of stores to be at before leaving town. She would leave home at four or five AM and not get back home until ten PM or later, depending on the size of the list. She would haul three gallon containers of ice cream in an insulated box Marvin had built. Then Friday mornings the whole family helped get the orders made up that were picked up the week before. This meant sorted and package for the weekly delivery to the lodge that had ordered it.

As busy as she was Willy Lou made it a habit, if at all possible, to go to the airstrip with her pilot husband when he was leaving. She'd help him clear the snow or frost off the wings, undo the knots on the tie-downs on the struts and tail wheel during the winter months. After the engine was heated and run long enough to heat the oil, the engine shut off and engine cover put on, they walked back to the kitchen for breakfast. They were up early and before anyone else showed up they sat drinking their coffee and talking over plans or a past days activities. Most of the time it was the only ten or fifteen minutes they had to them selves all day, because by the time he retuned late in the day, the lodge would be full of people eating or

Warbelow's aircraft a cathedral Bluffs.

milling around. She would walk back to the airplane with him and as he revved up the engine for takeoff he would roll down the window, wave and blow her a kiss. She'd wave goodbye, whisper a prayer to herself, "Please God, bring him safely home," then hold her breath until the plane lifted off the end of the airstrip, cleared the trees at the bottom of the hill and on into the sky and out of her sight. Then back to her full day's work.

As much flying as Marvin did he had his share of bent props and emergency landings and some times walked back before Willy Lou sent some one to look for him. He had always told her to give him twenty-four-hours before calling some one. She did her share of worrying but never waited that long. There was always somebody she could call. One time he was on the ground with a bent prop and it was her privilege to drive to Fairbanks to get another one, then locate a pilot with a floatplane to deliver it. The pilot she had called located him and the problem but was flying his airplane on wheels and couldn't land.

One time he was gone so long it had everybody in a panic, even the boys who always had confidence that their dad would handle whatever problem he was faced with and would surface in due time. August 7 that year, an early snow storm arrived and lasted five days. There were hunters waiting at the lodge to fly out to hunting camps but two women geologists out in the hills were the ones he was worried about. He had set out supplies for them during the summer, and was to meet them again at a designated place on the 12th.

The plan was to set out their supplies and return the same afternoon. He had been watching the weather and when it looked like it was clearing some-what he took off. The

Willy Lou, Cyndie, Ron, and Charlie.

ladies were waiting at the place they said they would be when he arrive. They were wet and cold. Everything was covered with snow and he chose a sand bar next to the river to land on.

It was snowing lightly when he landed and showed no signs of letting up. There was no way the girls could do more geology work and he felt he had to get them out of there. They climbed into the back seat and he piled their gear and back packs around them. Twice they helped him clean the snow off the wings while waiting for a letup in the snowfall.

Finally it started clearing slightly and he decided the time had come to takeoff. The sand bar was short, the plane overloaded and visibility was so poor he couldn't see the end of the bar. As the plane gained flying speed he tried to bounce it into the air, and on a second bounce it looked like they were going home, but a down draft caught the plane as it neared the hill close to the river, the wheels hit water and lost flying speed. Then it settled in the river with water flowing into the cabin, clothing bags and duffle bags floating out the open door and down the river.

Three days later all three miserably cold and weary people walked in to Chicken following an old cat-trail. From where they left the airplane tied to the bank, they had crossed a 5600 foot mountain (it was later named Mt. Warbelow) and had trudged more than thirty miles with no letup in the snow, rain and wind. Marvin had left his emergency gear and heavy clothes at home to lighten the load knowing the girls would have a load with them. Willy Lou had thoughtfully sent along some warm clothes for the two girls but every thing went floating downriver and no one could get out of the plane and to shore fast enough to retrieve any of it.

By late afternoon of the day Marvin had left and wasn't back Willy Lou knew he was in trouble. He had left in a light snow storm thinking it would clear as he got farther toward his destination. The storm worsened. It was two days before the pilots she had notified, were able to take their plane in the air to search. The three boys weren't home (not due back for three days). Cyndie was home with her and they shared their concern that he might be down and hurt with no help in sight. Regardless, a pilot will tell his wife to give him time to walk in from someplace, it is agonizing for the ones at home waiting and imagining all kind of things that could have happened to him.

At daybreak the third day that Mavin was missing, Bob and Ellis Roberts with their Piper Family Cruiser, and Bill Simmons with his Stinson, all from Tok, had their planes ready to go but violent winds kept them on the ground until late in the day. They located the Cub tied down in the Kink River but snow had obliterated all tracks and they had no way of knowing which way he went or if the girls were with him. They flew the areas the two had been working but no sign of a camp or them.

Willy Lou and Cyndie were close to hysteria faced with another long night of not knowing. About midnight the boys arrived home to hear all about their dad being missing. So much crying it took awhile to get all the details. The boys were panicky and had all kinds of theories as to what might have happened

"We got to get a plane in the air at daylight," Ron said.

It was close to daylight when Willy Lou called Bill simmons out of bed to tell him the boys were home and Ron wants to go with him. His answer was that he had to get a couple more hours sleep and would go again as soon as the wind laid. Four in the morning, Cyndie and Ron were in Tok where Bill had his plane tied down and when Bill arrived two hours later the plane was gassed up, ropes untied, cleared of snow and ice, fire-potted to heat the engine and it was ready to fly. They were back within a couple of hours with the news that all three people were within an hour or so of walking into Chicken. Everyone was exploding with excitement. Two airplanes were fired up to bring them back in style.

It is obvious that Willy Lou—a bush pilot's wife—can handle just about every situation she has been faced with. She handled a bear situation differently than most women would have. She was busy cooking in the cafe one summer morning when a bear walked right in like it had been invited for coffee. It had been seen around the place occasionally but never bothered anything. Not wanting to shoot it she took the broom after it. She was whacking it on the rump as it exited the kitchen and headed down the path just a Marvin and the four kids, returning from a trip in the woods behind the lodge, rounded the end of the building in time to see the bear get a good whack and scolding. They thought it pretty funny.

Marvin rolled down the window of the pickup and yelled, "the wrath of a woman."

One summer they had a large construction crew parked on their grounds. Some of the workers from the Lower 48, brought their families and they lived in trailers and motor homes. There was a lot of kids with them. One of the workers shot a young grizzly bear, loaded it in the back of his pickup and brought it to the lodge. Its head was hanging over the back and blood was dripping onto the ground. These kids from 'Outside' had never seen a grizzly bear and were terrified. The gory sight of the blood dripping out of its nose didn't encourage any one of them to get close. From then on it was that ugly 'Drizzly Grizzly bear,' There was grizzly and black bears in the area and in the near hills. These kids were all warned about bears and not to wonder away from the yard. That 'Drizzly Grizzly' was all that was necessary to make a believer out of any of those kids if he should take a notion to explore in the nearby wood.

Another year families with tents and campers set up house-keeping in the back yard. Marvin had put a fifty-five-gallon drum of water earlier in the season for the kids to dip water out of. The campers didn't realize what it was for, and dumped their garbage in it and it was a mess. A black bear cub had been hanging around the place and was quite tame. It was a real clown. Every night when the men were home from work, and it had an audience, the cub put on an act. He would jump up and hang onto the edge of the barrel with all four feet, stick its head down into the barrel and slosh around in that mess of water and garbage. He waited until he had a good audience around then let his front feet slip down into the mess far enough so his whole head and shoulders were covered in it. Then he would pull himself out and with his head all covered with garbage, look around to see how his audience was enjoying his antics. It was obvious he enjoyed their laughter and they laughed until he went into the woods to roll and clean himself up. Next night he'd show up about the same time. They never seen him again after it was time for him to go into hibernation.

That same summer, Andrew Issac from Dot Lake worked for the crew so he and his wife Maggie set up a tent in the trees across the road from the lodge. There had been a large black bear show up around camp a few times and all the fellows on the crew were hoping to collect it come hunting season. It had a thick black fur, and would make a nice rug or mount. The cook in camp was sure he would be the one to collect it because he was in camp all day and kept his rifle close. He was quite the sight when he was out in the woods wearing his white coat and chef's cap, carrying his rifle, looking for that bear.

Maggie Issac would go over to visit Willy Lou every morning after Andrew left for work. One morning when she went over to visit, she sat awhile then calmly announced "I shoot a bear!" Willy Lou thought she misunderstood her and asked what she said.

"I shoot a bear this morning. I was still in bed after Andrew left and I heard a noise and sat up in bed and that bear was standing in the tent door. I took the pistol we keep under the pillow and I shoot it dead. The boys come help me pull it out of the door way so I can skin it," she answered.

"There were a lot of surprised men in camp that evening."

At Cathedral Bluffs they were connected with telephone service but had their own Witte generators for power. Two of them and one was a backup. They had to be hand cranked and the boys could hardly wait until each one was tall and strong enough to crank it. Ron was the first one then Charley then Art. They felt real grown up when they achieved that goal. That time came and went fast. They were growing up fast and soon it was their responsibility to hand pump the fuel from the fifty-five-gallon drum into the Witte fuel tank, as well as the equipments' tanks. The boys also helped their dad overhaul and maintain the Wittes, car motors, equipment motors, aircraft motor and repairs, change from wheels to skis on the plane and vice-versa. Cyndie was a busy young lady helping her mother with the endless chores required to run a roadhouse.

All of the children went through their high school with courses from the University of Lincoln, Nebraska. Mother still supervising. Cyndie went on to graduate from the University of Alaska in Fairbanks. A year later she received her Masters from the University of Michigan.

Willy Lou's help was still needed when Ron graduated. She drove to the college to get him and a whole load of whatever it is that kids accumulate in a dorm room during four years of college. Her main concern was his family of fish. He had two aquariums full of exotic fish plus heat lamps, pumps and thermostats.

In 1970, tragedy struck and the three boys had their plans for college canceled. Marvin had just finished his lunch and went to the shop to spray paint the airplane he had been working on all that morning. Then just minutes later a deafening explosion in the shop. When everyone in the lodge ran out to the shop, Marvin lay on the floor with paint and blood all over him, unconscious and badly injured from metal bolts and pieces of the paint pot that struck him in the head.

The compressor was upside down on the floor, and the exploded paint pot lay on the work bench, paint covering everything. Marvin was so badly injured he never recovered. It was a terrible time for Willy Lou and the children. They had always been together as a family to share the joys, the hardships, and the worries when husband and father was overdue.

The day the accident happened, all three of the boys were home and helped to deal with the crisis. Cyndie was called home, and all of them kept things going at the lodge for the eight months that Willy Lou drove to Anchorage, on the average of once a week to be with him in the hospital while he was slowly dying. He never regained consciousness. Icy winter roads didn't keep Willy Lou from the three-hundred-mile drive. They had been married twenty-five-years.

Willy Lou with a grandchild.

The three sons carried on there father's air service, and made flying there careers. They were: twenty, seventeen, and fifteen-years-old when there father died. All of them took flight training and the tests with no problems. After they had their pilot's license they moved to Tok and started a flying business under the title: 'FORTY MILE AIR.' At a later time Ron had a helicopter service until he was a victim of cancer in 1995. Art owns WARBELOW'S AIR VENTURES in Fairbanks. After FORTY MILE AIR was sold, Charlie was killed in a helicopter crash in Portland, Oregon — November 1999. He was in Portland to bring back a helicopter he had bought for his new business. Cyndie and her husband own greenhouses, and a country store on the Chena Hot Springs road, a few miles out from Fairbanks.

Willy Lou moved to Tok and some years later married Dale Young, a business man in Tok. They had a second home on the Island of Hawaii. A few years later Dale Young Died of a sudden heart attack. She now has step children, as well as many grand-children, and all are included in her close knit family. She has kept herself busy writing, and now has six best selling books.

After Willy Lou's sons had their own flying services, she was visiting relatives in Wisconsin and she decided she wanted a log book of her own to show her boys when she returned. A nephew made arrangements with his instructor to give her a few lessons. He told the instructor that his old gray haired aunt was down from Alaska and has a lot of money and wants a legitimate log book with a few hours of flying time entered in it. No stalls or solo was to be understood. Take her up and let her fly the airplane around a few times. As a result she had a log book with two-point-six hours logged in it to show her pilot sons on her return.

LeNora's added comment to Willy Lou's story.

After Marvin Warbelow died and they were moving to Tok, Bud Conkle bought the Caterpillar bulldozer from them. I went with Bud to haul it to Eagle Trail Ranch. He was expecting some one to be there who could help him load it on the two ton truck. It was siting alongside the house and nobody home. He took the blade off and would make a second trip back for it. As was his usual way of doing things to get the job done, he rigged up planks he found and when driving that heavy piece of equipment up onto the bed of the truck, the plank next to the house cracked and had it broke the Caterpillar would have crashed onto the side of that nice house, Willy Lou's first home. I think the only thing that saved it was Bud pushed onto the gas peddle to move it faster onto the truck and took a chance on it going over the cab. He often amazed me with his courage to do some of the things he got by with. Ironically, it was the motor on this same bulldozer he was starting to crank when he had the heart attack that was brought on by the strenuous things he had been doing

Chapter Fourteen

Elaine Smith

E laine Messer was born in Bartlett, Texas. Her father was a cotton farmer. Eventually she moved with her mother and older sister to Austin, Texas. She went through her school years and graduated from high school in Austin. After graduation she got a job with the State Health Department in Austin. It was while working there she met Hardy Smith who was employed there also.

Hardy enlisted in the US Air Force in 1942 and while he was a Cadet in training at the US Cadet Academy in Colorado. Elaine took a train to Denver and they were married May 1, 1943. In 1944 Hardy was stationed at Stockton Air Base in California. While she was with him in California their first daughter, Linda was born. Elaine went back to Austin when Hardy was transferred to Germany. It was in Austin there second daughter, Carol, was born.

The war had taken Hardy Smith to Germany in 1946 where he participated in the 1948-1949 Berlin Airlift as a pilot with the American Forces. When Peace was declared he sent for Elaine and the girls to join him in Germany. At that time she was living with her mother and sister in Austin and had relatives and friends near by. They hesitated in encouraging her to go to war-torn Germany, where emotions ran strong after such a terrible war.

Quoting Elaine's daughter Carol:
Nevertheless, my mother was a woman with spunk and determination. She had the pioneer spirit even then. She went ahead and got all the required shots for herself and the two little girls, one-half, and one-and-one-half years old, packed up all their clothes and diapers, caught a train to Fort Hamilton, New York (a

seven day train ride). The Red Cross met her there with open arms and she stayed there fourteen days while getting the required paper work in order and awaiting the ocean going ship they would travel on to Germany. June of 1947 they boarded the huge ship for a ten day ride to Bremerhaven. On their arrival in Germany they took a train to Frankfort where Hardy met them. It had been a 30 days adventure—showing determination and real courage.

(Returning to Elaine's adventures in her writings): In March of 1948 (after a short stay of only eight months), she and the toddlers returned to the United States on Pan American World Airways.

December of 1948 (some twenty two months later) Hardy

Elaine Smith

returned from Germany and was stationed at Patterson AFB Dayton, Ohio and then on to Elgin AFB in Florida. In 1956 he was reassigned to Elmendorf AFB in Anchorage, Alaska. Elaine and the children would stay in Austin with her mother if no on post housing was available at the many Air Force Bases where he'd be transferred to, and would join him whenever housing did become available. They now had two more children: a girl Nene, and a boy Mark. Both born in Texas.

In 1963 Hardy was stationed at Clear, Alaska for a short time and then back to Kelly AFB in Texas where he received his discharge papers from the Air Force. At the time Elaine could not accompany him to Clear, Alaska. But would soon be making her permanent home in Alaska, as Hardy had been hired as a pilot for Wien Air Lines.

April of 1964 Hardy and the two girls, Linda and Nene, drove the Alaska Highway to Fairbanks to find housing and start his new job flying for Wien Air Lines. But on arrival he found Wien had not planned on him starting work for another month. Wien gave him air fare back to Texas and he left the two girls in charge of the trailer house he had rented in North Pole, and the car for Linda to use (she wanted to look for a job while he was gone). He planned to bring Elaine and Mark, and all the household goods they could, back with him. But Elaine and Mark had already left for Alaska! He now was in Texas and she was on her way to Alaska.

Elaine and Mark left Helotes, Texas, 15 miles from San Antonio, to drive the highway to Alaska. She drove her Volkswagon Bug (which the two of them ate and slept in) all the way to North Pole, Alaska with the exception of one short night in a motel. Only one incident occurred; one night a pickup truck had pulled up behind them, and bumper to bumper, was pushing their car. She woke up, flashed the lights and they drove away). A Volkswagon isn't a big car and when it was loaded with all the groceries and soda pop they would need on the trip; sleeping bags, clothes, skillet and dishes, extra tire and tools, there was not much sleeping room. They had one flat tire on the whole trip and that happened in Canada, luckily near a place where she could get it repaired.

Even as late as 1964 the Alaska Highway (Alcan), was no freeway. May weather was unpredictable, roads still gravel and dusty (or mud) most of the way, gas stations few and far between as well as houses and towns. But to make the trip from Texas to Alaska in eleven days, with $20.00 in her purse on arrival after departing with only $150.00, took some good finance management. Besides being brave enough to head for Alaska with her eleven year old son so they could all be together as a family. Elaine had the courage to go to Alaska to join her husband and to drive the Alaska Highway to get there. Daughter Carol had stayed behind with family living there, scheduled to come later (she stayed to finish her high school). Hardy flew for two years for

Wien Airlines then retired in Alaska. He and his brother, O. J. Smith, started a hunting business; bush type flying and taking polar bear hunters (as passengers) while flying out from Kotzebue and Barrow. Elaine, with her background, growing up in Texas in a hard working family, was a natural for a bush pilot's wife. As a pilot's wife she soon learned to cope with the fact he'd be gone for days at a time on various hunts, sometimes on a rescue mission or a mercy flight, and if the weather was bad and he had no way of letting her know, she just had to wait and hope. But those years he was away (in the military) prepared her well for her new life in Alaska. After O. J. and his wife Elly, started their own business at Umiat, Hardy and Elaine moved into their modern home and it too was in North Pole. In both places she had a telephone and with the VHF radio in his plane they always had good communications.

In 1965 Elaine worked at Ft. Wainwright as a clerk-typist in the Plans and Services Division. When she retired in October of 1988 she received a Letter of Appreciation and a thanks for a job well done.

Elaine liked to fly with Hardy, but would get airsick and that took away all the pleasures. All the kids flew with him at various times. Linda and Carol married and are now in the Lower 48. Nene and Mark were the ones he took hunting. Nene shot a polar bear when she was only eleven! Also went aerial wolf hunting with her dad and shot a wolf from his airplane when she was in her early teens. Mark (the youngest), also shot a polar bear when he was only 13! Hardy enjoyed taking them on the ice packs with there uncle O. J. flying cover for them.

Mama had confidence in Hardy's flying ability, but couldn't train herself not to worry when the kids went on those serious hunts when weather or unexpected conditions could, and usually did happened. She just had to rely on her faith that all would be well and would be relieved when everyone returned safe.

She was the only one who had an emergency when her husband was away from home flying and not due back for many days. She had to have a gall bladder operation. Hardy was where he could phone and called often until her recovery. Soon she was home again.

She had been able to handle all the other things that happen or go wrong when the man is away.

Chapter Fifteen

Eleanor "Elly" Smith

Eleanor "Elly" Quick, born and raised in Missouri, moved to Idaho. Later she enlisted in the air force. While stationed at Kirkland AFB in New Mexico she met Oliver J. Smith, better known as OJ. Both had duty assignments in the 'Block House,' a secured area. His office was in the Electronic Counter Measures section (ECM), she worked in the control center. She was eating an apple the first time she met him.

"How about a bite of your apple?" he grinned as he asked.

Feeling embarrassed she immediately left the coffee-break room.

She loved riding in airplanes and would ask the pilots that worked in her section, to go with them on their occasional flights. She had been doing this so often the pilots would call to let her know when they had a round trip to other bases. One day OJ called to let her know that a flight she was planning to go on was canceled, but he was flying that day and invited her to go with him. She jumped at the chance to go. Not because it was with him but because it was flying in an airplane. There were many flights with OJ after that.

"Nearly fifty years later, I still preferred to fly with him than riding in a car with him driving!" she'd say.

OJ Smith was born in Llano, Texas and they were married in Austin, Texas. OJ served at many bases during his air force career … some overseas. The family joined him at the stateside bases. Jay was born at Keesler Air Force Base, Mississippi. Jacquelynne was born when they were stationed at Ardmore Air force Base, Oklahoma. Ray was born at Ladd Air Force Base in Alaska. OJ was transferred to Alaska and during his off-duty hours he was hired by local air taxi operators as a pilot. He also became a hunting guide.

Their first home (the term "home" used lightly), was in a small community south of Fairbanks—12 Mile Village (a short distance from North Pole). This frame house had three rooms with a small addition attached bathroom. The water source (a well), was plumbed to the bathroom sink—the only sink in this 'deluxe' abode. The sink was very small, allowing only a quart size pan under the cold water faucet. There was no hot water. Water temperature coming directly from wells in this part of the country is around 36 degrees F. The toilet didn't always flush. The shower was simply a shower stall standing in the corner of this small structure and was of no use because there was no plumbing to it. The living room and kitchen were combined into one room. The dining table was the only working, or eating, surface above the floor.

Wooden crates served as a stand for the two-burner Coleman stove used for cooking and heating water. By using a small pan to catch the water from the bathroom sink, pouring it into the galvanized tub in the shower stall, then letting it set until it warmed to room temperature, proved a faster method than heating it a little bit at a time, if the cooking pots, coffee, laundry or water for cleaning didn't take preference.

About three times during the winter, the family would go in to Fairbanks for a steam bath and do laundry at a laundromat. A real treat! It was a good thing they didn't have a lot of furniture then because of the needed space for the "workshop" purposes. It wasn't wise to leave tools outside in the cold.

Elly soon learned how to dismantle a Herman Nelson space heater and put it back together. They had three of those heaters, but seemingly only one at a time was operational. The other two were laid up in the workshop. Herman Nelsons were portable, fuel burning heaters used to warm aircraft engines and interiors and to thaw out the family vehicle sitting out in the cold winter months, because of no garage. They were also used to thaw out the plumbing and sewer systems. In the game of preparing a car for travel—before turning the key, it was important to warm the interior of the car, or airplane, so the instruments and gauges would work. The "workshop" was also used as a butcher shop for cutting up and packaging moose meat.

There was a gravel street in front of the house and a bush type airstrip through the willows behind the house. They had a car, a Super Cub and a weasel equipped with roll bars - an army surplus tracked vehicle — these were the open-air type. The closest telephone was a mile away. No need to worry, In those days neighbors relied on each other for assistance, or messages. Going to the store was a real outing.

The beautiful, long summer days gave Elly and the family, the needed change from long winter months, also a change from a winter diet of the Alaskan native beef—moose meat, a bountiful garden of vegetables, brilliant flowers and fishing trips supplemented this diet

Summer was also a time for upgrading their home, equipment and vehicles. The real luxury for Elly was the hot water heater and plumbing installed. The heating system rerouted to include the shower stall. By the time another son—Ray was born they had enlarged their home by adding a living room, and kitchen with wall cabinets, sink and the work shop relocated to the garage, which they now had. What luxury! All of the work done by OJ and Elly.

Many times Elly had expressed how grateful she was for having grown up on a small dairy farm where she learned how to take care of and repair equipment, mend fences and outbuildings, deal with floods, fires, snowstorms and whatever the weather sent their way. "Our farm house burned down when I was five years old. We lived in the hayloft of the barn for several months that winter. About ten years later I helped my father build the farm house that is still in the family, and still being lived in."

When OJ established his guiding business, Elly's training as a guide's "grass widow" began. Fortunately as an air force wife, she already had military wives training while he served in Korea and Formosa. Between all his flying and guiding on the side, he wasn't home much. Once while away, he missed a bad flood at 12 Mile Village when people were forced to evacuate there homes. Elly sent the children with a neighbor and she stayed to protect what she could, or to help others in a variety of situations. The next year a tundra fire threatened the village and caused another evacuation. OJ was gone again, and again she sent the children away with a neighbor, and stayed. All those who stayed hooked up garden hoses and kept the roofs of theirs and neighbors homes hosed down. The military bases joined the forestry units in getting the fires under control. Small burns, singed hair from tree sparks and smoke inhalation was all the damage she and others suffered. There also were others not so fortunate!

When the power company notified them they would no longer provide service unless they were on a electrical circuit breaker system, she inquired about how this could be done and a friend who had upgraded his own system, wrote out the instructions and Elly was able to install her own circuit breaker system. This required the running of electrical wire through a conduit and under the house to the master switch board. It passed inspection and they had power by the time OJ returned home. Bush Pilot's wives, more than in other professions, have to deal with all types of situations and emergencies because they seldom live in modern communities.

When they needed to put in another septic system, their friend Bud Hilton told her how to do it, the kind of utility to construct, what type of pipe was best to use and how much of a "in-line drop" the pipe needed to get the best flow. She built an insulated box over the septic tank and cesspool so-as to have access at 40 below (if necessary to pump or thaw the system). That system is thirty-five-years old and still working. She was real pleased with herself for those jobs well done and appreciated the help from those who told her how.

What Elly did find difficult was scheduling her time to be away from home and the kids when OJ had free time to teach her to hunt and use a rifle. Her first real hunt came about when she drew a permit for a special cow moose hunt. A friend of theirs also drew a permit for the same hunt. OJ was guiding a hunter for other game and couldn't take her. A friend offered to take her and Bob in OJ's weasel. They came back with two moose and it had really been a workout. In all the rush to leave on the hunt they left the axes and knives home and had only a single 4 inch blade to gut out their moose. To do a job of this magnitude with this kind of equipment, you simply remove your coat, roll up your sleeves and reach up to your arm pits into the rib cage through the slit you have managed to cut through a tough moose hide with a pocket knife. The other end isn't so complicated. Your friend's help is welcome. The second moose went faster because their gutting technique had improved. Lastly, hands and arms are washed with snow before rolling down your sleeves and putting on your coat. The work has just started when they get home and these large animals have to be butchered and packaged. Elly hadn't stood back to watch the men. She had shot her moose so she was obligated to help do the rest of the job too.

Because Bob had snow packed in his gun barrel, Elly shot his game for him. On returning, it seemed they were the only ones who had harvested their game that last day of the season. She was elated until returning home and found a very unhappy husband. She had taken his guiding rifle and he was delayed on his scheduled hunt and had to end up guiding the hunter with his shot gun. It wasn't easy to convince OJ she had shot two moose on her first hunt. That Christmas Santa brought her a fine BSA .30-06 rifle.

After OJ's Air Force career, he did a lot of flying for some of the air-taxi operators and some flight instruction. Some times Elly could go with him and study the maps, checking with him for her accuracy in tracking their position. There is a lot of muskeg, rivers, forest, mountains and valleys out there. Roads, villages and towns are few and far between. Some of the bush flights she went on were a bit more exciting than the usual ones.

One of the trips to Canada (hauling produce), Elly went with him. On takeoff they experienced a brief electrical "hot shot." OJ turned off the "culprit's" switch, and the smoke soon cleared, but the odor in the cockpit lasted awhile. Later it was discovered some of the electronics were no longer functional, but that old Bamboo Bomber's twin engines were running smoothly. However, getting the retractable landing gear to operate was a bit of a chore. They landed at Ft. Yukon to fuel up and check the weather. Weather between Ft. Yukon and Fairbanks can change fast. Leveling out over the flats with the landing gear only partially retracted, OJ told Elly to take the wheel, keep the plane level, while he hand cranked the landing gear up. It took awhile and soon they were into turbulence. It appeared they were nearing a "black wall" (pilot jargon), where there is a vertical wall of weather (usually rain and wind). The weather moved in and was clear to the ground. Her map following intelligence paid off at this point, for by the time OJ was back in seat flying the plane, visibility was grim. She showed him the last position she recognized on the map. He was flying blind for a very long 30 or 40 minutes then they broke out over the foothills north of Fairbanks. She didn't say anything other than, "It sure was nice to get out of that weather".

Driving home OJ said; "You were too stupefied to be scared."

"Thank you honey, I indeed was scared out of my mind, but I saw no sense in cluttering up your concentration with how I felt," she answered. With that answer they both laughed.

While working for Wien Air, one of OJ's stations was at Umiat, Alaska. That is a location, not a village. A runway was built with a support camp as a staging area for oil exploration. It was the only airstrip on the North Slope until the DEW line (Distant Early Warning) sites were constructed. At the time, the three kids were in grade school so Elly stayed in North Pole until their school was out, then they moved to Umiat. While in North Pole, and the kids in school, Elly worked at the 12 Mile Bar. The house they lived in belonged to the owners of the bar. She also sold ads for the *Fairbanks Daily News Miner*.

They would spend their summers and holidays in Umiat. It was very remote … in the foothills north of the Brooks Range on the Colville River and about eighty miles south of the Arctic Sea. In the spring, a real variety of water fowl flew by stopping at the many ponds and small lakes near there. The peregrine falcon nested in the bluffs south of there and just across the river. Ptarmigan were in abundance. Arctic grizzly bear dens were close. The caribou migrating back to the coastal areas came passing close by. Wolves, wolverines, foxes, ermine, voles, lemmings and the short tailed ground squirrels were everywhere. Moose browsed on the abundance of willows along the river bed. Wildflowers bloomed … and mosquitoes hatched. The kids loved their life there.

The Umiat Fall is beautiful when the brush turns so many different color. Carpets of cranberry and blue berry bushes spread out in areas like a patchwork quilt. The first hard frost cut down the mosquito population to Zero. A great relief from the "clouds" of them during the summer months when a head net and repellent were the desired attire and "cologne" of the north. It was also time to harvest moose and caribou. The caribou herd, migrating south, came through the Umiat area in the fall.

The first Thanksgiving OJ was stationed at Umiat, he sent Elly a message to cook a turkey dinner and bring it with them. They boarded the Wien Air plane with pans of roasted turkey, pumpkin pie, cranberry sauce and the total dinner including home made bread fresh out of the oven. Enough for the crew of six men based there at that time and their three kids ages eight, five and three.

The living quarters at Umiat were primitive in a quonset hut. Running water was getting it from the river. Winter time meant cutting a hole in the ice for water. Toilet facilities, of course, the-little-house out back. Elly scrounged an old cupboard and other items she made use of that she found in a warehouse that had been left by the Civil Engineer or the Navy or Air Force during their occupancy. The Wien employees started saying, "there goes Elly building a nest." It was near Umiat that their son, Jay age eight, harvested his first caribou.

There were three barrels behind the heating stove in the middle of their home. One held ice, the other held melting ice. The third held water almost warm. One of the men from the camp made a barrel with a spigot to sit on a frame over the heating stove. Results;...running water! The framework had caster rollers so it could be pushed, with the barrel of water out of the way while cleaning, and servicing the stove. The refrigerator was small, but necessary to keep things frozen. OJ would take most of the laundry with him, and do it at which ever site he stopped, if they had laundry facilities. Sometimes it was four days before he was back with the laundry, so it took planning for Elly to keep them in clean clothes. The washboard didn't have the opportunity to get rusty.

They had a Super Cub and a Cessna 180. On one of the polar bear safaris, a friend and his brother in their airplane, OJ and Elly in their Super Cub, headed north to the Arctic ice pack to harvest polar bear. On passing Lonely, (a DEW line sight on the coast), their friend's airplane had an emergency landing with major engine trouble. OJ had earned his A&P license during his early years in the Army Air Corps, determined the engine would have to be taken out for repairs. OJ and Elly flew to Camp Lonely, borrowed tools and took water to freeze in the tie-downs, stripped the Cub of all the extra gear and weight so the two place plane could carry the two extra passengers, left a message they would gain enough altitude so they could be tracked on radar back to Umiat.

Back at Umiat, Elly's comment as the guys at camp helped them all out of the Cub, "Those two guys and myself were crammed behind the pilot's seat. There were knees under my arm pits, feet beside my elbows and my knees up around my ears. We were a bit cramped. They found it amazing that we were all able to cram into that small airplane."

Every place they went it seemed like there was a tent, an old quonset hut or cabin which Elly would fix up so they could stay in it. One time they all went to Naknek for awhile where OJ had an old cabin that leaked and there was nothing on the windows. There was a rusty old stove in it. Elly and the kids scrounged enough stove pipe around the area to pipe the smoke outside and a bit of this and that to put on the roof so it didn't leak. By the time she and the kids were all bit up by the plethora of white socks, OJ returned from a trip with cheese cloth to cover the windows.

One day their dad took all three kids and a tent to go fishing in a stream where they planned to stay overnight. It rained, the tent leaked and the kids wanted to go home to Umiat. They were used to roughing it but only up to a point.

While at Umiat, Elly took the kids fishing at a stream where another creek poured into it. They were chasing salmon around and getting too far out. Elly was on the bank and terrified because the tide came in so fast and they wouldn't be able to make it to shore and she wouldn't be able to get to them. It was one time she felt totally helpless, but the kids heard her yelling and barely made it back to shore ahead of the rising water. They had been having too much fun to think of anything but those darting fish.

OJ flew for Wien Air for three years and was transferred from Umiat to Kaktovik on Barter Island, two miles off the northeast coast of Alaska about sixty miles west of the Canadian border. There, (as Elly expressed it) they nested again. She fixed up an old, small, quonset hut for them to live in. The children went to the Bureau Of Indian Affairs (BIA) school. When asked why she was living there she told them, "So the children can at least watch their dad sleep once a week!" Flying the Defence Early Warning (DEW) line, did not give him much time to be in any one place for long. They lived there for three years in the late sixties.

Winter winds there were frequent and fierce and the days dark when the kids went to school. When the winds came up, Elly would leave a light on in the new window and with the wind at her back, she would make her way to the school, tell the kids to hold hands and follow her all the way and not to turn loose even if one fell down. Fortunately the direction of the drifts were constant in their location. They just got bigger, sometimes drifting over the roof of the quonset hut they lived in. They counted the drifts they climbed over so they would know when to make a right turn and follow that particular drift home. They never saw the light until a few feet of the window. The children were great there, no fussing or crying, seeming to find life here more exciting than frightening.

Because clothing left on the floor overnight would freeze to the floor, with the children's help, Elly built shelves for their toys and clothes. The cooking stove was from an ancient trailer house. It had three burners so small and close together that only two medium pans would fit at a time. Baking bread was a challenge because of temperatures in the hut and the oven would only hold one loaf at a time. For a table they split a four-by-four foot piece of plywood down the middle making a two-by-four-foot table. To get the proper height, the kids sat in chairs and the height that was comfortable for them was where we marked the wall to show where to attach our new table.

At the start of the school year, the following fall, one of the teachers didn't arrive. Elly offered to be a study hall overseer, but on arrival that first morning she was assigned the four upper grades to teach; fifth, sixth, seventh and eighth grades. All the kids loved her as their teacher and she was sad to leave when the new teacher arrived. In school she was Mrs. Smith, her two boys included. But at home she was still "Mother."

Elly and the kids participated in the Koktovik Winter Olympics. The competition included a Ladies Shoot. Framed and on her wall is a very special "medal" made of recycled items. The "medal" is bigger than a silver dollar and is made of card board with a beautifully drawn rifle with a scope, in the middle. Attached to it is a band of blue crepe paper with two stripes of yellow ribbon hanging from it. Neatly printed by hand it reads; "LADIES SHOOTING CONTEST FIRST PRIZE" 1967. What an honor for Elly, especially after one of the ladies had given her the three shells she needed to compete.

Everyone participates in those Olympics. Because they were new and untested, they were the last ones to be chosen to be on respective teams. The Smith children proved to be good in sports and were chosen to be on the various teams long before the end of the games.

For entertainment they skied behind the snowmachine, set fox traps out on the sea ice and went to movies shown occasionally at the DEW line site, located on the small island.

While they were living at Barter Island, transplanting operations of musk ox from the west coast to the north eastern corner of the state was taking place. The entire family participated in moving the animals to the mainland and working with the Fish & Game personnel assigned to this task. Their job was to check on the welfare of the new arrivals (animals).

There were many exciting and challenging experiences while living at Kaktovik. Elly learned from the native women how to take the hide from the legs of caribou and made the upper part of mukluks and clean and shape the tough hide of the walrus for the soles.

Winds that are constantly blowing at thirty knots were considered calm for Barter Island. By the second winter they were acclimated to them. At times the stronger winds moved grains of snow, and hard packed snow into any little crevice available. As an example: One morning some one opened the door to let the dog out and there in front of us was a solid wall of snow. OJ had to knock part of the porch roof off, then shove the dog up through the hole, then each kid, so they could go to school. Wind had drifted the snow clear over the quonset hut.

In the spring they harvested polar bear, bringing in the meat for their neighbors and in the fall they harvested caribou sharing the meat with the village. In the summer they fished for Arctic Char in the bay and off the western spit of the island. In the bay they set out a net which had to be pulled often because the tiny shrimp would eat the Char entangled in the net. Those "ocean trout" are delicious. They had a Weimaraner dog that had been in the family for eleven years and went with them everywhere, in the airplane, on the snowmachine or racing alongside it, and in the boat. He would dive into the water and grab the fish, bringing fish and the net to the boat.

Their first winter at Barter Island they were out on the ice with the snow machines. The dog running along with them did not see a hole where ice had been cut out and he slid on his haunches trying to stop but slid into the icy water hole. Elly and kids were upset thinking it would drown but she grabbed his feet and pulled him out. They took him home and dried him off and warmed him up and other than being embarrassed, no after effects.

When Wien Air left the Dew Line flying operations, they moved back to North Pole. While Elly was packing up and getting ready to move, caribou were spotted on the mainland. Ray, the youngest son, was determined to get one before they left Barter Island. His brother Jay, had gotten one when he was eight years old and Ray felt he could too.

When her son Ray shot a polar bear, he had to stand on a chunk of ice because he was so small he couldn't see over the ice ridge to see the bear. She boosted him up until he could sight in on it. Elly told him where to aim, and when he pulled the trigger, the first bullet hit a fatal spot. Jay had shot a polar bear when his dad had taken him out on the pack ice. Not to be outdone, Ray insisted he be taken Polar bear hunting also.

OJ had flown to a site on the West Coast, where Elly phoned to tell him she was loading up the camping gear and Snowmobiles to take Ray for a caribou hunt and they were not going to leave there until he got one.

While they were loading up one of their neighbors told a cousin who decided they should not go alone. Their safari ended up with four snowmobiles, two sleds loaded up with camping gear and six kids, ages between nine and fourteen. Ray shot a trophy caribou and the safari returned with four caribou to share with the village.

While the Wien airplane was loading all their possessions at Barter Island, (the DC-3 was stuffed with household goods, kids and the dog), nearly all the village came to bid them goodbye. When the aircraft door closed, tears came. It was like leaving the family. They had grown fond of the people there.

After they moved back to North Pole, Elly and the children started working on a produce farm during the summer. OJ retired from Wien Air and started flying and guiding for a small charter business. Then in May 1975 they started their own business in Umiat - UMIAT ENTERPRISES. OJ was happy with this new adventure and so was the family. They all loved it there. When they moved back to Umiat their youngest son, Ray said, "gee dad, this is paradise."

The hunting and guiding business kept everyone busy. Elly went out on the ice pack to help skin the polar bears their clients shot. She cut up the meat they brought back to give to the villagers. The native men finished preparing the rough hide. Out on the ice, the head and feet were left on the hide. The bloody hide was then dipped in sea water, through a hole cut in the ice, until it was clean, then tromped in the snow, rolled up, and while still frozen, shipped to the taxidermist.

One morning one of their clients intended to go on a polar bear hunt, but had indulged too much the night before, and didn't feel like getting out of bed. OJ told Elly to get ready and he would take her instead. By sheer luck, one big old boar polar bear was wondering out and about. She returned with the largest polar bear taken by any of their clients that year. A real trophy.

Elly was so much a part of their business she was involved in every aspect. She filled in at times as an assistant guide for some of the hunts when they were short handed. One day OJ sent her and five Eskimos and their two boys, out with snowmobiles, to bring in a wrecked airplane that was left on the Canning River. A project that took them two long day.

While they were living at Umiat and OJ was flying for Wien Air, Elly had worked as a stewardess for Interior Air. OJ would volunteer her services when they were short handed. And she ended up flying with them for one year until the family moved to Barter Island. She also dubbed in as a ticked agent for Interior Air. Those flights went to Fairbanks, Anchorage, Clear and Barter Island. They were not all scheduled flights, and most were short trips so she wasn't gone from home overnight. She earned a reputation as a gal who tolerated no nonsense. On a flight to Utopia Creek, a smart-aleck passenger pinched her on the rump while she was serving coffee. She turned and whacked him with a punch that took him by surprise. Then she went up to tell the pilot, "That guy is getting off the plane or I am!" When the plane landed the guy staggered to the door and, before the stairs for passenger unloading was wheeled into place, he stepped out into space and fell ten feet to the gravel runway. One of the ground crew yelled back up that he was still alive. Needless to say, he wasn't a passenger when the plane took off.

Elly was flying with OJ one very cold day in their Super Cub and the can of mosquito repellant (that was always carried in the plane), rolled unnoticed in the turbulence and alongside the heater. It got too hot and exploded with a loud bang. They were flying over open tundra and OJ took a chance landing at the first place he thought he could set down without serious damage to the plane, or them. He was thinking it was the shot gun that had gone off and was expecting to see Elly covered with blood. After OJ helped her out of the plane he was happy to learn there was only bruises—thanks to the heavy winter gear she was wearing.

"With all the flying you have done, how come you didn't check to see if anything came loose in that turbulence? You let me make an emergency landing where I might have wrecked the plane and us to!" he said, while wiping the sweat from his brow. No comment from Elly.

Along with her many skills, she also was proficient at flying. She had taken flying lessons, soloed, and could take off, and land with the Super Cub or the Cessna 180. But time didn't allow OJ to finish instructing her to get a pilot's license. He wouldn't allow anyone else to instruct her. He wanted that privilege. She preferred it that way and enjoyed the times she could fly with him as the pilot.

May 2000 was the Silver Anniversary of the business at Umiat. Both sons are also pilots, and along with their mother, still operate UMIAT ENTERPRISES. OJ's last safari was July 1999. Their memories of him and the good times they had as a working-together-family, dull the edges of missing him.

Chapter Sixteen

Mary Frances DeHart

Mary Frances Pew, was married to Don DeHart, who was a noted big game guide and outfitter, but he wasn't a pilot. He used horses in his outfitting business. They were married in Ohio where Mary Frances was born and grew up.

They returned to Slana, Alaska, mile sixty-five on the Tok highway, where his established business was located— The Hart DeRanch.

Although Mary Frances's husband wasn't a Bush Pilot, she was a woman of the same caliber—her work would have been considered equal to that of a Bush Pilot's wife. She had a registered guides licence, took care of the horses, cooked in hunting camps, drove the tractor towing a trailer loaded with camping and the hunters gear, miles from the ranch to the foot of the mountain where they had an established hunting camp. This was across roadless muskeg and swamps in back country. She skinned the trophies, and prepared them for the taxidermist, and whatever else was required of her.

Several years after they were married, Don DeHart was diagnosed with Parkinson's disease and hospitalized for months before he died. Mary Frances continued to run the hunting business, did some of the guiding of hunters herself, setting up all the camps, overseeing these camps and hired guides, booking the hunters, did all the book work and correspondence.

Eventually she sold the horses and quit the guiding business and went back to what she was trained for. She had been a grade school teacher, but her real talents and interests lay along artistic lines. She started training and learning to work with bronze. She became very proficient at the skill of working with bronze and was a talented artist. She soon had a going business selling her wildlife bronzes, as well as booklets of Alaska's birds and animals. She is still living at the Hart D Ranch and has since added an RV park and a bed and breakfast type Motel on the property. She took complete control in supervising the construction and completed most of the finish work herself. She does all her own repair work on the Generators at the ranch, the caterpillar tractor, plowing snow to keep the driveways open, and since her mother's death, is the postmistress for the Slana post office, which is located on the Hart D ranch property. Yes, it is felt by this author, that Mary Frances has the qualities and heart of those of a bush pilot's wife.

Chapter Seventeen

Helen Lee

Helen Merrill was born and raised in Umatilla, Florida. It was in the first grade of school she met Alfred 'Al' Lee. He also was in the first grade at that same school. They were friends all through their school years but didn't date until they both had graduated and after he returned from service in the US Army Air Corps. It was there he learned to fly. Soon after his return to Umatilla they would get together Wednesday nights after Prayer Meeting and choir practice.

Helen and Alfred "Al" Lee.

After six months of dating, they were married. Five months later he told her of his interest in going to Alaska. In mid June, they packed up all their belongings, (not very many), in a ton and a half Ford truck pulling a beat-up little house trailer, and headed for the Alcan Highway and Alaska. The arrived in Anchorage, July 13, 1947.

Soon after their arrival and they had time to get settled, Helen went to work for the Air Force as a surplus property clerk. Al worked construction on and off the two military bases, Ft. Richardson and Elmendorf AFB. In their spare time they built and finished several houses. Helen learned a lot about the different trade: carpentry, plumbing, electrical work, as well as the financial part of buying materials and selling. At that time she had given some thought to a career as a carpenter.

Helen with Al's trapping success—wolves and lynx.

While they were living in Anchorage they had two children, a daughter Patricia and a son Jerry. Al receive his commercial pilot's license, as well as his temporary instructor's license while in Anchorage. Patricia (Trish), was six years old and Jerry was four when they made the decision to move to their present location—at mile 158.5 on the Glenn Highway, thirty miles west of Glennallen.

At this location they had applied for, and received, a Trade and Manufacturing site (T&M). They built their home, with an airstrip, and became qualified for title to the land. They had a floatplane base there also. They started a guiding service, LEE'S AIR TAXI, with Lee doing all the flying, outfitting and guiding. Helen cooked for the hunters and guides, kept the cabins clean and habitable for the clients, picked up hunters on arrival at the

Anchorage Airport, transported them back to their lodge then returned them to the airport when their hunt was over. While in Anchorage there are always groceries and accessories to buy. She also kept the books and did considerable amount of maintenance around their place. Besides being the good mom to her kids, she had to drive them to meet the school bus in the morning and again in the afternoons after school — five days a week, because they lived so far from the highway. Both children went through there school years in Glennallen.

While living in Anchorage they owned a Super Cub, and a Piper Pacer, then traded both for a new Super Cub. At a later date a Beaver was added to the business.

Lee had given Helen flying lessons while they were still living in Anchorage and she had soloed. She took the airplane up by herself a few times, but soon decided to leave the flying up to her husband. He readily agreed.

Most of Al Lee's flying and guiding business was in the Glennallen area and mountains of the interior. He took hunters for early spring and late fall hunts on the Alaska Peninsula. Helen says she is not sure whether she worried more about him when he was flying from their home base, or when he was down on the Peninsula for a month or longer, and for short periods of time she could forget that she had a husband. Al did a lot of trapping in those first winters, and his trapline was so extensive that he checked his traps using his airplane. Helen always helped skin the animals he brought back.

One cloudy, bleak evening he didn't return. There was not much sleep that night for Helen. Along toward noon the following day, his plane flew in to land with a small spruce tree holding one ski on. His explanation went as such; "In the dim light, a ski had struck a snow berm hard enough to break the ski leg. It gets dark fast at that time of the year, and Al had to camp over night where he was. In the morning he jerry-riggd the ski contraption, then flew the plane home. Fortunately there was small trappers cabin on that lake, with a small cabin heater stove. Al took the stove out and used it to heat the airplane engine to get it started (at forty-below-zero).

Helen always enjoyed flying with her husband (when he wasn't too busy with customers). It didn't happen often, as he was usually too tired, and it was usually late when he finished his working day to do much pleasure flying. She did get to spend a little leisure time at one or the other of their cabins on Crosswind Lake. She enjoyed those outings and liked to wander around and spend time on the lake shore watching the ducks that spent their summers there. In the early years she was too inexperienced to realize how many bears also wandered around in those woods. She never encountered one in those woods, but without the Lord watching over her, it might have been a different story if she had met a mean one that could have cut her off between cabins when she had taken walks without the rifle.

One morning Helen was talking to a neighbor on the phone, while looking out their front window she starred into the eyes of a grizzly bear, who was looking through the glass right back at her! At the time the weather was good and the kids usually walked the one-quarter-mile home from the school bus on this same road. Also there were hunter's wives in the yards and the guest cabins near the main house. One wife was paralyzed from the waist down and in a wheel chair setting out side of her cabin. Helen felt it best to do away with that bear! As fearless as that bear was to come right up to the house in broad daylight, he wasn't a welcome guest. The paralyzed woman heard the shots, but couldn't see the bear. Another woman was in the kitchen canning berries and came running to see why the shots?

The Fish and Wildlife officers, however, took a different view of her actions. For awhile it looked as if she would be having her board and room paid for by the State. The magistrate threw the whole case out of court. Helen Lee decided it wasn't real smart about her phoning the Department of Fish and Game about the demise of that grizzly bear. The Fish and Game biologist came out from Glennallen and took the carcass away.

When their daughter Trish was out of high school and son Jerry was a junior, Helen took a job with the Department of Labor as an Employment Interviewer in the Glennallen office. Al's hunters were mostly from out of state. They normally stayed at the base lodge just long enough for Al to fly them out to temporary camps in the hunting areas that had a cook in camp. Helen's responsibilities to the hunters was now limited, she could do most of what had to be done on weekends. Her routine 8 to 5 job included many varied duties. This enabled her to travel around the State quite often. Finding jobs for people (and vice versa) was gratifying for her.

Late 1991, Evelyn Bunch sold them an aircraft hanger on Tolsona Lake. It had been the late Ken Bunch's base of operation. Helen's duties now were even more limited. She'd answer the phone, all personal inquiries, keep up the correspondence, do the book work, and make sure there was food at both locations, which was a problem, as she never knew which location Al would choose for his meal. She was always a busy help-mate in their business.

Their son Jerry is a pilot now and a partner in business with them. Now, Helen has two pilots to worry about. She confesses; she is a worrier, she worries and prays for Al and Jerry both when she hasn't anything else to do. There have been many times one or the other of them have been long overdue, but only once did it happen that both were overdue. They had flown to the Arctic, to an isolated area some where in the vicinity of Kotzebue, to repair a downed airplane. Severe weather kept them grounded, although the weather reports had been reporting favorable flying in the Kotzebue area. Helen spent three long days and nights worrying and praying until her husband and son returned home safe. Weather where they were at had kept them grounded and out of radio range.

Late September 1995, Rosemary Bartley, the wife of a neighbor pilot at Snowshoe Lake, mile 147.3 (neighbors in that area are folks who live close enough to reach within the hour), phoned for Al. She told Helen that her husband was overdue from a flight to Tazlina Lake to drop off some sheep hunters. Weather was bad but Bartley (Bart), had his Cessna 182 and said he'd come right back if it was too bad to land at Tazlina. When he was much too long overdue she had Dennis Pollard, a pilot who worked for them, fly the Super Cub to the lake looking for him but couldn't locate him, so returned to Snowshoe Lake. The wind was too strong for the Cub on Tazlina Lake, and he couldn't do much flying there. Al wasn't flying that day, due to the high wind and turbulence, but was at their floatplane base twelve miles north east of their home base. Helen called Al. He said he would crank up the Beaver, and fly over to Tazlina to see if he could locate Bartley as soon as the wind gusts subsided.

Helen didn't know that the hunter, who was waiting at the hanger for the weather to improve, went with Al. For three hours Helen and Rosemary were in constant telephone contact, waiting for any word coming back from the search planes. Al had radioed back that Bartley's plane was spotted upside down in the water with Bart was sitting on a float.

A BLM helicopter, flying in the area, heard the call for help and in their rescue attempt, came too close with the landing skids, striking Bartley, breaking four of his ribs on one side, and five on the other, one having punctured his lung. This also knocked him off the float into the water. Then a rotor blade on the chopper plowed into the water. This flipped it over into the water and it began sinking! Her son Jerry returned from a flight while Al was still gone, and he left immediately to fly over the scene of the accident.

"All I could do was pray hard for everyone involved. Rosemary and I both knew the hazardous situation all these men were faced with and we knew that all may not survive," Helen said.

Now there were three people and two flying machines in the icy water. Al Lee, of LEE'S AIR TAXI, who had just arrived, was flying over the scene, made the decision to land the Beaver on three-to-four-foot waves on that dangerous lake surface. By sheer strength, experience and luck (and with the help of Helen and Rosemary's prayers), Al taxied the Beaver close to the half-submerged floats. He managed to keep the Beaver steady enough for the two men from the helicopter to get the badly injured Bartley aboard. It took all of Al's skills to taxi that plane to the nearest shore, where they built a fire, and waited for the National Guard helicopter that was in the area. The NG picked up Bartly, and flew him to the Alaska Regional Hospital in Anchorage.

Helen, of course, was grateful for answered prayer for the lives of all those men. Al was awarded a Carnegie Medal from the CARNEGIE HERO FUND COMMISSION in Pittsburgh, Pennsylvania in recognition of an outstanding act of heroism.

Helen is still a busy lady, involved in many community and church activities, along with her husband and son, and the business they still operate, and two flying machines.

Chapter Eighteen

Rosemary Bartley

Rosemary Tacciacore was born and raised in Chicago, Illinois. It was while she was working on a job in Chicago that she met Clarence "Bart" Bartley. He was a Corporate Pilot for Big Bear T.C. Industrial (tractor contractors), in Chicago.

They were married in Chicago in 1972 and soon after, they moved to Tennessee, and lived there for ten years. While in Tennessee, Bart flew for various Commuter Airlines and some private companies. Rosemary worked as a secretary for two of the companies.

In May 1989, they bought Snowshoe Lake Lodge and the hunting and charter business it was involved with. Snowshoe Lake is located at mile 147.3 on the Glenn Highway, forty miles west of Glennallen. There they had an air taxi business—ALASKAN AIRVENTURES. In their business they owned a Cessna 182 and a Super Cub. Bart did most of the business flying with the Cessna, unless the Super Cub was more suitable for the flight and the landing conditions. Guest cabins were already there, they came with the property and were always in use during the busy hunting and fishing seasons.

Rosemary first worked as a teller at the National Bank of Alaska in Glennallen, and later as a secretary for the Copper Valley Electric in Glennallen. She kept the grocery supply shelves filled at the lodge by driving round trips to Anchorage on weekends. She did a lot of the cooking or preparing the meals in advance, if and when the hunters or fishermen were weathered in and waiting at the lodge to be flown out to their camps. Fishermen usually brought their own groceries and cooked for themselves in their cabin. Hunters were fed in hunting camps.

Cabins had to be cleaned for the next occupants. Rosemary did this after her normal work day at Glennallen.

The Bartleys were noted for their hospitality. It wasn't long until business kept him busy flying and she was needed at the lodge where she kept a busy schedule. Everything was going well for them over the years, until that eventful day on September 10,1995, when Bart left Snowshoe Lake to take two sheep hunters over to Tazlina Lake. It was a routine flight and Bart was to set them out on the shore, on the far side of the lake, close to the sheep hills where they would hunt.

The wind gusts there were strong but nothing he hadn't flown in before. He knew the Cessna could handle it.

Rosemary started getting concerned when too much time had elapsed and Bart hadn't returned or called her from the airplane radio. She had always felt comfortable with the radio communications they had. He was faithful in calling to let her know if he was delayed at any time or place. Dennis Pollard, a pilot working for them, was also concerned and volunteered to fly the Super Cub over to Tazlina Lake. Bartley's plane was not at the northwest side of the lake where it should have been and the two sheep hunters had already left, probably on their way to set up their camp at the foot of the sheep hills. He had no way of knowing if they had arrived there or were still with Bartley. The winds were too gusty for that light Super Cub to do any further flying over those miles of open water and high waves of that big lake. He returned to Snowshoe lake, then Rosemary phoned their neighbor pilot, Al Lee, to ask if he would fly over to locate Bart. Al said he'd go as soon as the wind gusts let up a little.

When Bartley hadn't returned back at Snowshoe Lake to pick up the other hunter, a friend, Chuck Atwood, grew concerned and asked two other pilots, in two other airplanes, to begin searching the twenty-mile Tazlina Lake. One of the search pilots spotted Bartley's plane upside down in the water with Bartley clinging on one of the floats. High winds and three foot waves discouraged fixed-wing aircraft from landing to attempt a rescue.

From the time the first radio message was sent back to Rosemary from the search plane that spotted Bartleys downed airplane, was a three hour anguishing ordeal for Rosemary. Especially when word came back that there was now a helicopter, and two rescue men also in the water! Rosemary knew there was only a very slim chance her husband would survive, but her faith never wavered. She fervently prayed and waited. She knew from the radio messages the chances Al Lee was taking in his rescue attempt. She wondered would he also become a causality.

Bartley, later in a interview with the *Copper River Journal*, told them that the winds got worse, and the weather indeed turned out to be a serious problem. He had aborted a takeoff, after setting the two hunters out on the beach, and to play it safe, taxied five or six miles to the southeast (lee) side of the lake, out of that stiff wind. Bartley had been in that cold water seven hours from the time his plane flipped over until he was pulled into Al Lee's Beaver.

Besides the article in the *Copper River Country Journal*: September, 1995, published out of Glennallen, the *Anchorage Daily News*, September 12 1995, also wrote up this rescue. Then *Alaska Magazine*, October 1999, and *Readers Digest*, January 2000, also carried this story.

Footnote: Bartley's Cessna 182 is still on he bottom of Tazlina Lake (awaiting salvage). It had been a good airplane.

Chapter 19

Lena Gregory

I was born, at quite a young age at Akiak, Alaska on the Lower Kuskokwim River. My father, Arthur Laraux, originally spelled L'Heureux, was from St. Marie, Quebec, Canada. A mink rancher, he was out feeding his mink when I was born at home with my grandmother attending my mother.

Both of my ancestral lines had always lived close to nature and they took things as they came without much worry. From birth we were taught, mostly just by example, that when we started on a trip to anyplace, long or short, to think well ahead and prepare for events we knew we would encounter and think of all those we may encounter and make allowances for them. As a result, when someone was a day or two overdue on a trip with dogs, snowshoes, or even just on a foot trail with a pack and rifle, we weren't overly concerned unless the time became excessive or a severe storm had occurred. Even then there was almost always a logical explanation for the delay. To us, worry came in the category of too much effort and not enough progress.

Before the airplane put in an appearance, travel was restricted to dog teams or horses in winter and boats and canoes in summer. By the time I could remember, airplanes were a common sight to us. They were accepted with open arms both summer and winter. As young children, we recognized, occasionally talked to, and eventually rode with many of the pilots. They seemed to be a fixture, associated with some sort of an undiscribed romance, who just appeared with no particular schedule so we were never surprised to see them and never worried about when we would see them again.

During WW II my brother, Arthur Jr., was in the Army Air

Corps. He traveled over much of the world and sent home presents from places he had visited. I have a beautifully carved teakwood jewelry box, that I highly cherish, which he sent to Mother from Karachi or Calcutta, I don't remember which. At the end of the war, he was killed in a plane crash in the Bay of Salerno. He was on his way home. I was young enough that I did not comprehend the finality of the event. He had been gone from home for several years and I don't think it affected me concerning feeling anxiety for those returning after being away from home.

As my schooling advanced and it became necessary for me to leave home to go further, I moved to Bethel, also on the Kuskokwim River, to attend school. I stayed with various families, one of whom was Lew Browne, a brother to Nat Browne who was a prominent bush pilot in the area. As a result, I was privy to many conversations about engine problems, bad weather, poor airport conditions, and so many other things that could, and did, affect the flow of air traffic that I assimilated a built-in lack of concern for delays, at least until something concrete divulged a more sinister circumstance.

While I was staying with Clarence and "Bergie" Marsh, who ran a cafe in Bethel, my sister, Bessie, worked for Alaska Airlines. At that time Alaska Airlines had many bush stations and Bessie worked at the Bethel station. She, among other duties, operated the HF[1] radio which had come into vogue all over Alaska. The airplanes all had a set whereby they could talk to each other, as well as the ground stations. Those radios all worked on the same frequency and at times it was almost impossible to get your message through but that also created an atmosphere of camaraderie enjoyed by everyone involved. We all knew what the weather was like in King Salmon, Kotzebue, or Kodiak.

Many homes along the rivers had radio receivers. They could, and did, listen to that air traffic to the extent that little news otherwise arrived in any of the villages as a surprise. Many messages were passed along—some would make the Federal Communications Commission workers cringe but they were practically powerless to control it so it just endured until new VHF[2] radios eventually replaced the old HF sets and they just died a natural death. Many of those messages, if challenged, could be justified anyway, so striving for tight control was rather futile. Messages such as "John has a broken leg, we need an airplane," or, "We need a case of Clorox to clean the community hall for the big dance Saturday." Translated, that means, send us a case of whiskey.

The first of January, 1951, Glenn Gregory arrived in Bethel as mechanic for Northern Consolidated Airlines (NCL). A short while later George Thiele also arrived to fly for them. The two of them shared a room at the roadhouse which NCL owned. Both of them would often be very late completing their duties so they would come over to the cafe to eat supper. Often the cafe would actually be closed but we would find them something to eat. During regular hours they could order instead of having to eat at the established time when the roadhouse served family style.

Mary Lou Marsh, daughter of the owners of the cafe, was about the same age as I. Of course we didn't realize those two may be coming to the cafe for any reason other than to eat—until George started teasing me abut Glenn. (He would also go back and tease Glenn about me.) You have seen pictures and heard stories about Cupid?

To spare the reader the details of a dignified courtship I will simply state that Glenn and I went to Fairbanks and were married in June of 1951. We were scolded severely for getting married in Fairbanks because that "beat" the people of Bethel out of a big party. George and Mary Lou were married later that same summer.

Glenn left the airlines and went to work for Morrison-Knudsen construction company at Campion, a small radar installation and airport a few miles above Galena, on the Yukon River. While working there Dominic Vernetti persuaded Glenn to stay in Koyukuk, just below Galena, and fly trappers for the winter. I stayed at Akiak with my mother until my father returned from the mines at Nyac, then flew to Koyukuk for the winter.

Had I been a professional worrier I could have plied my trade to a high degree that winter. On one occasion Glenn went over to the Kaiyuh Hills to move a trapper. During the move he dropped a ski into a water-hole covered with about ten inches of snow, right out on the flats where one would never expect it to be. He was alone. The trapper had gone with the first trip of the move. The airplane didn't have enough power to pull itself clear of the hole so the only thing he could do was close the throttle and let the airplane settle back into the water. With no other help available it was necessary to get the airplane out of the hole with brute strength and horsepower. His solution was to tie a rope to the throttle, lead the loose end to the spot from which he could push, reach in and give the engine full power, then run around the airplane and the hole to the top of the wing struts, grab the rope, lift and push for all he was worth. After the ski cleared the edge of the hole, he closed the throttle with the rope. The procedure worked but after getting out of that overflow his left ski was caked with snow and ice. The temperature was -30 degrees so the performance of the airplane was very good but with ice on one ski it was difficult to taxi and keep the airplane running straight on takeoff. Most important, however, it was time consuming to operate with that handicap and he had already lost about 45 minutes just getting out of that hole. He didn't return to Koyukuk until after 10 PM. I was concerned, but clung to the knowledge that there was a logical explanation for most delays. I did sit alone quite a bit that winter. I like needle work and I like to read. I also like to listen to my husband breath deeply as he sleeps while I sew.

Another time, just before Christmas, all the trappers wished to be home for Christmas. They all wanted to come in as late as possible in order to not lose too much time from the trapline. The bringing in of the trappers started off very well and on schedule. He went to Huslia the evening before he was to start bringing the trappers to that village. His plan was to stay the night thus getting an earlier start but the next morning the entire country was covered with fog. The fog persisted for three days but did break on December 24. He picked up the Huslia trappers then started on those still out on the Yukon. He was down to the last two but almost out of daylight. He went to one camp and saw another pilot, Donald Stickman, had come to pick up those two, but they were unable to get their loaded airplane moving. Glenn stopped to help, planning to then go on to his last trapping camp. It was very cold which caused his engine to quit when he throttled down. He landed in deep snow, knowing the boys on the ground could help him get turned around. He would help them get started, then he could get moving since he was empty. The only trouble was they worked too fast turning the airplane. A hard pull on the rope put too much strain on the landing gear causing an axle to break. They all made it home, but the point is: even with those problems, those fellows would always seem to figure out something that should work, and it usually did, so that was another factor that helped me to not borrow trouble or worry—too much.

I had an ability to recognize different airplanes by their sound. That was not a difficult thing to do when you were comparing a 300 hp engine with one of 85 hp, but I was able to develop the ability to distinguish the airplane Glenn was flying from an identical one flown by one of his pilots.

Especially while we were at Koyukuk, I could always hear him as he approached the village even if he came straight in for his landing on the ice out front. The night he walked into the house and I hadn't heard him, I knew something out of the ordinary had happened—I knew he had not flown his airplane home. It was dark in the hallway and he would not step into the house where I could see him. He kept telling me he was not hurt, he had just worn out the airplane and had to walk home. Well, he was hurt. He kept kidding me and insisted on something to eat. He had a bad cut in his lower lip. His collar bone seemed broken and he was so sore he couldn't lay down in bed. He sat on the bed and we let him down gently to a prone position and he didn't stir all night. Ella Vernetti, wife of the local trading post operator, administered local first aid to all comers so she did what she could for him with what she had for supplies and equipment. That was limited to about a Band-Aid over his lip and a sling for his arm to take a load off the collar bone. Bill Carlo, a miner from Ruby who flew his own airplane, came into Koyukuk the next day at noon and took him to Tanana to the hospital. I was at home, alone, except for visitors and began to occasionally entertain the thought that my baby was coming soon. However, so far in my young life, things had always worked out and I was sure they would again.

After a few days in the hospital he was released and went on into Fairbanks, bought another airplane and returned to Tanana. He rode into Fairbanks with Alden Williams, an old friend who was flying for NCL. He told Alden to bring me into Tanana on his next flight. He told Alden that the birth of our first child was near.

On his next trip downriver Alden sent me word to be ready

when he came back and he would take me to Tanana. At Tanana Glenn had made arrangement for me to stay with Frank and Mardella Coil. Frank worked as a communicator for the Civil Aeronautics Administration. When the day arrived I had waited too long to tell Mardella and couldn't walk to the hospital. She pulled me up to the front door of the hospital on a children's coaster sled. That was the beginning of a lifelong friendship which continues to this day. They eventually reared eight children as did we.

The Deputy U. S. Marshall, Frank Wirth, was the only person in Tanana with my blood type and Dr. Wehler felt he needed to replace the lost blood if he could, so I became marshal of Koyukuk—by transfusion.

The temperature was -40 degrees when we took the twin daughters home to Koyukuk. Glenn was flying the newly acquired Stinson Gullwing which had a very minimal heater but we just wrapped those babies up as we would have for a trip with a dog team. Frank Wirth held one and I held the other and they slept all the way home.

Glenn was flying for NCL and was in Aniak replacing Reinhold Thiele who was on vacation, when our next daughter, Vicky, was about to be born. He had asked the chief pilot if he could be stationed in Fairbanks, at least until the baby was born. He was given leave when Reinhold returned and our daughter came along without a hitch. He never did get any word about a new station so he went to work for the building contractors at Eielson Air Base. Later that spring Don Hulshizer came to see if he wanted to fly for Wien Alaska Airlines. He had not felt very appreciated while working for NCL so he was reluctant to again fly for a subsidized airline. He liked to make decisions and try to have the airplanes make money but found too much government interference while working for a scheduled airline. He recommended our friend, George Thiele, who took the job but Don came back again a few months later—just to see if maybe he had changed his mind. Well, the construction season was well advanced so a possible winter flying job sounded inviting—he took it. The first station was Barrow, then Bettles, then Barrow again. While at Barrow he sent home some caribou meat and from Bettles he sent home a huge moose. I had begun to think perhaps I should just keep him out there.

While Glenn was flying out of Barrow I was stranded at home with a perfectly good car parked in the yard. Gean Starkweather was staying with us, living in our basement apartment, so I asked him to show me how to shift the gears. I taught myself to drive and would sneak into town, do my shopping then return home. As I got a little braver I would go a little farther into town. All worked out well and I was not so homebound.

At freeze-up at Barrow Glenn, could not get through the mountains to Fairbanks, so he took the floatplane to Kotzebue to keep it from being frozen in at Barrow. He planned to over-night there, then proceed to Fairbanks. It just happened that Kotzebue station needed a C-170 on floats and wished to trade their Norseman on floats for it. Fairbanks management agreed so he flew the Norseman on into Fairbanks. From there he was sent to Nome to replace Johnnie James while he was on vacation. I took the twins and went to Nome on the Douglas DC3 to spend a week. We enjoyed the stay. While in Nome I went into the Commissioner's office and took the drivers written test. He didn't even give me a driving test but issued me a license.

Glenn was then transferred to Kotzebue where he replaced Thomas Richards while he was on vacation. When Thomas returned the flying was still so heavy that Glenn was kept for the rest of the winter. He was given notice that he was now on permanent status after successfully clearing all hurdles of the beginner pilot.

About a month later, Sig Wien, president of the airline, was in Washington D.C. The Civil Aeronautics Board (CAB) told him to cut down one pilot. Glenn was that one pilot. Our fourth daughter, Lolita, was born that April. That summer Glenn flew for Larry Rost on a Coast & Geodetic Survey contract. The next summer he returned to working for the building contractors. Marquita, our fifth daughter, was born that fall.

Later Glenn was flying out of Barrow for Interior Airways. Neither of us cared for the separation, especially when some of the girls were not sure who their daddy was when he did come home. He gave notice that he would be leaving the first of June. I was never worried about his flying as I heard none of the war stories that grow from such quarters and I had enough little ones at home to care for that I didn't have time to worry. We had five little girls at that time. All but the twins were born in the old St. Joseph's Hospital in Fairbanks. Fortunately, Glenn was home, so far, when all the babies were born.

When he returned to Fairbanks our friends, the Conkles, were rebuilding a Piper Cub and they wanted him to help them. Glenn always said they could have done it easily without him but he understood that confidence building affect of having a person there who had done it before. That acquaintance moved right into the next chapter of a wife sitting home and waiting for word or the return of her man. In this case the wait was not long.

Bud Conkle flew that rebuilt Cub for a couple of years then bought a new Super Cub with a 150 hp engine. That considerably increased his ability to go and do the things that he had been almost able to do previously. At the end of one season he landed on a lake with ice too thin to hold the weight of the airplane and it broke through. Glenn went out to help retrieve the newly baptized Cub but it was apparent they needed more equipment. The ice was now of a thickness that Glenn could operate there with his Stinson so he loaded up a barrel of gasoline, his tools, a Herman Nelson heater and Jimmy Anderson for the quick retrieval. I heard them go roaring up the runway which was only about a half mile straight across the river from our house. I could tell they were in the air but when I heard the engine suddenly stop and then heard the crash, I knew. I waited, and waited. Apparently nothing bad had happened or someone would have called by now. Really, I guess it was not such a long time, but it did seem so. Finally Eldred Quam called to tell me what had happened and to say that nobody was hurt. I told him that was about what I had figured.

Glenn said several times that losing that Stinson was a blessing in disguise. He had a full set of instruments in it and he was ready to take his check ride for his instrument rating. After losing the Stinson his written examination time limit expired before he was able to get organized to take the flight test so he said, "To heck with it." He didn't need an instrument rating to do the flying he was doing and didn't plan to again fly for the airlines. Later an instrument rating became necessary and he had to start over. The flying and studying he had to do to qualify for the rating was a wonderful education and update. It seemed that stateside flying was catching up to the Alaskans.

After we moved the operation to Tanana and opened a trading post, we acquired one of those wonderful time savers: A Northern HF radio with which we could talk all over Alaska. Glenn could sit on the ground at Northway or the mouth of the Yukon and talk to me in Tanana. I was able to contact him in the air and divert him to business that had not yet materialized when he had departed Tanana. Several times I was able to relay very important messages to the Alaska State Troopers he had as passengers.

One thing that made me more anxious than any other thing I encountered during the entire time we were rearing children surfaced soon after we arrived in Tanana. One of the young single men got a little fresh with me after he had been drinking. Of course I told Glenn but he didn't say a word. About a week later he was in conversation with that young man, who was now sober. Glenn broached the subject. Of course he admitted he was probably a little out of line but it was because he had been drinking. Glenn told him that excuse was absolutely unacceptable to him since it was his experience that most people did or said things when they were drinking that they didn't have the nerve to do sober. There was no more problem from that quarter.   •

Another fellow had established that when he got drunk he often mistook the home of someone else for his own, broke the door down and raped someone. One evening Glenn was in the store and a bunch of the fellows were in conversation. That subject came up. Glenn stated that he kept a loaded shotgun at the top of the stairs. If anyone broke into his house he would shoot and ask questions later. He also emphasized that he had given me training and instructions to do as he had outlined. He explained that it was his position that he had a wife and seven daughters to protect. If that fellow had a problem when he was drinking he was aware of it when he was sober. He was sober when he took that first drink which meant that he was totally responsible for what he did later. Of course the word spread. No one knew whether or not Glenn was serious but you can bet that no one really wanted to find out either. Later, when the warden of the federal prison at McNiel Island wrote and asked Glenn if he would recommend parole for that fellow, Glenn told him that as far as he was concerned the man was right where he belonged and the longer he stayed there the better it would be for both

him and the community. It was several years before he was released and he never did come back to Tanana to live.

We were really fortunate as far as health and accidents were
concerned. Glenn was home during the only times that I may
have been sorely pressed to do everything by myself. When the
first five girls had their tonsils removed, all at the same time,
Glenn was there to help. We were at the receiving end of the
chute when the doctor removed the tonsils and turned the unconscious tots over to a nurse. We took over when she dashed
back to catch the next one. After the first ones began to awaken
they were moved into another room where I took care of them.
Glenn stayed at the receiving chute. After our children were
attended to, the young ones just kept coming. We cared for
three more young ones who had donated their tonsils to the
cause that morning. We didn't even see their parents, nor did
we get paid for our professional services.

Stephen was born while Glenn was finishing a season of
construction work. He took a short job running dragline for the
Alaska Road Commission and dropped me off at the hospital on
his way to work. Stephen, number six, was the one impervious
to cold. When he was quite small he went with his dad and
Harold Esmailka to help a neighbor set up some chicken houses
and feeders. It was October and cold. One of the tubs of water
had about $3/_4$ of an inch of ice on top. Stephen took off his
parka and worked on that ice with his fist, his heel and finally
resorted to a rock to break the ice, then played in the water.
When he came to his dad, with is nose dripping, his hands
turning blue and stated he was beginning to get cold, Harold
thought he was the toughest kid he had ever seen. That tendency prevailed. When we were in Tanana we had few pets but
did have a couple of dogs which Stephen fed each night. He
would go out barefooted to feed his dog regardless of the temperature and it was not just to show off as most of the time it
was dark and no one could see him. Once we went fishing at
Melozi (the Melozitna River) across from Ruby. We borrowed
Harold's boat and caught some huge shee fish. When we retuned to Tanana we were informed that Stephen had been exploding some .22 cartridges by placing them on a rock and
striking them. One exploded in a way that sent shards of brass
into his leg just above his knee. He just calmly walked down to

the hospital and asked the doctor to make it new again. I didn't worry about things over which I had no control.

Zoanne was born while Glenn was working at Clear Air Force Station. I called him in the morning and told him that Mike Agbaba was taking me to the hospital, then called later in the day to announce that he was now the father of a new baby girl, Zoanne Elaine.

Myrna was also born at St. Joseph's hospital one evening. Glenn took me over and waited until she was born. My child bearing years were now behind me—I hoped.

During the time we were rearing eight children it was necessary to mix business with pleasure. We started each of those girls tending the store at the age of twelve years. We let them know we had confidence in them that they could do it and urged them to figure out the solution to problems they encountered. We usually didn't have to correct their decisions but on some occasions we did point out how it may have worked better had they done it differently. The main thing we kept in mind was their decision had been made with what they had to work with at the time. They made it sort of a game.

The girls took turns helping to clean the house, the store and to prepare meals—all were talents that would really be a benefit to their future husbands. As adults, they are all good decision makers with confidence. Some have expressed their gratitude for the training they received in that store. We will not tell them that training came in the form of help badly needed that we probably otherwise couldn't have afforded at the time. We also usually knew where they were and what they were doing.

Occasionally it became my unpleasant duty to pass along sad news. Virginia and Edgar Kalland also ran a little store in Kaltag, about twenty minutes below Galena, on the Yukon. I had met her while on a trip with Glenn and had occasionally talked with her over the radio. Her mother was in the hospital in Anchorage. Her brother, Ambrose Kozevnikoff, worked at the hospital in Tanana. Her mother passed away and the information was passed along to Ambrose who asked me to call Virginia and inform her. When I called, Virginia answered, "loud and clear." I gave her the message as gently as I could. I heard a carrier as though she had keyed her microphone and then nothing more. I called a couple more times, then repeated the message in the blind. (I just transmitted the message, hoping she would hear it.) I really felt bad, thinking that perhaps I had not delivered the message as gently as I could have—it bothered me. Some time later Virginia told me that when she started to acknowledge receipt of the message the transmitter blew a fuse just as she keyed the mike.

On one occasion Glenn took a nurse, Mildred Yoder, from the Tanana hospital to Anuktuvuk Pass to check on some sick babies and, if necessary, bring them back to the hospital. The

Lena helped with everything including stripping velvet from moose antlers.

nurse recognized Spinal Meningitis and insisted upon seeing every baby in the village before leaving. They strung out the trailing antennae for the HF radio and called me. I called Dr. Miller on the telephone. He approved her decision to bring a covey of babies back. It was -40 degrees and that airplane had been sitting several hours by the time she finished. Glenn ran the engine to keep it warm but he was familiar with ice building up in the breather tube, especially in an idling engine, so before they left he shut the engine off, then tightly installed the engine cover. The heat from the engine thawed the ice that had formed. When they removed the cover he told me an icicle about 18" long slid out of the breather tube. Knowing that he was aware that such problems could possibly form helped me to not be too concerned when they were a little overdue. Precautionary time well spent saved them much time traveling on snowshoes.

Speaking of babies—once we got a call from Nulato, about ten minutes below Galena, asking us to come pick up some babies for some reason. We didn't know the problem or the number of the babies so I decided to go along. It was after normal business hours, winter time and, of course, dark. We took the Cherokee Six which had five adult seats besides the two we occupied. We don't remember how many there were but the airplane was full and we had a seat belt over all of them. They were just as quiet and well behaved as they could be.

I must admit that there were times when I wished Glenn was in a different profession. Few were the Thanksgiving or Christmas dinners that we were able to eat and then relax afterward. Usually about turkey carving time the phone would ring and he was off on another emergency with a turkey sandwich in his hand.

One thing that helped me immensely was that Glenn refused all the charters to the North Slope when everyone got excited about tremendous discoveries British Petroleum had made. Glenn was very skeptical. The presence of that oil had been known for years. The Navy had drilled and proven oil existed in much of the North Slope. Oil companies didn't make huge disclosures of that sort. They tried to downplay discoveries, especially if they were of considerable extent. He felt the oil companies were trying to put pressure on the far east producers to get a better lease or something of that nature. At any rate, not long into the huckel-de-buck flying and drilling, everything was suddenly shut down and many operators, who had bought and leased more airplanes, went bankrupt. We just kept right on doing what we had been doing. It still scares me just to think about the turmoil that would have existed if he had taken off to the North Slope for weeks at a time.

One trip, on which I was a participant, took place a couple of years after Mr. and Mrs. Les James died in Hughes. They had a trading post and home there which none of their children wished to continue running. Jack Coghill, administrator of the James' estate, suggested he and his wife, another couple from Nenana and Glenn and I, go over there and look the place over for the purpose of establishing the value for the estate.

After the inspection was done and the real business completed we went on up the river and landed on a gravel bar to try our luck fishing. We caught no fish but established that those were the finest of landing areas for airplanes on wheels.

Several weeks later we decided to go up on a Sunday afternoon just for the sake of a break in the routine. We took several of the children and Libby Eller, a close friend of one of the girls. We again stopped at Hughes and conducted some small amount of business then flew on up the river and landed at a likely looking place to fish. After starting the engine at Hughes Glenn mentioned that the engine hadn't started as it usually did, perhaps he had flooded it.

We fished for a while, catching nothing, so we looked for odd rocks and just wiled away a few hours enjoying the sunshine, peace, and quiet. After we had all looked at each of the different rocks a few times we loaded up to go home and the engine would not start.

Glenn, with many years experience as a mechanic, was a good trouble shooter. He came to the conclusion that the magneto was not firing the spark plugs. Lolita was his little helper so he loosened a spark plug wire, grasped it in his hand, grounded the heel of his hand on the engine, stood clear of the propeller and told Lolita to hit the starter. That magneto was as dead as it could be. He first thought about taking both magnetos off and changing them around to make the starting magneto function, but the closeness and congestion of the wires, hoses, and engine mount tubes of the installation on the Cherokee Six caused him to change his mind. We waited and hoped.

We were sure we would have to spend the night so we began gathering firewood. We had a fair pile assembled when we heard an airplane coming. Glenn ran out and flagged him down. It was Sandy Hamilton, from Hughes. He took Glenn and Myrna, the youngest, back to Tanana to get the other airplane. He left instructions for us to assemble two piles of brush and get some gasoline ready so we could light the two piles of brush, one at each end of the area where he wanted to land. It was quite dark when we heard him coming and as soon as we saw the lights of the airplane we lit the fires. That gave him something to line up on and his landing light was sufficient for a good night landing. We all returned to Tanana. He took the bad magneto to town where Eldred Quam replaced the points and made it new again.

A couple of personal experiences of that nature help to emphasize the reasons one should not get too worked up about a pilot being a little overdue at times. Although it is hard, on occasions, to not be anxious.

There was one time, after the twins were grown, that gave me a few anxious moments. The twins were named Lois and Dolores. Lois was called Robin because, as a baby, she would lay on the bed, stomach down, and push up with her arms. Her little head would bob, much as a robin bobs while hopping across the lawn or listening for bugs or worms. That intrigued me so I started calling her Robin. The name is still with her. Dolores was called Dolly.

The twins had gone away to college when Robin decided to go on a mission for the LDS Church.[3] When the mission was completed she returned to Tanana in August. The leaders of the church in Fairbanks set a time for her to attend a meeting and report on her mission. The time was late one evening, which meant they would be coming home in the dark. That, in itself, was no big deal as the weather was fair and Glenn had much experience flying in the dark. After all, if a person is going to fly in Alaska in the winter time, he had better be proficient at flying in the dark.

Late August and September are probably the darkest months of the year. The sun, by then, is going far enough below the horizon to give little light. If there is no moon, it can be quite dark since there is, as yet, no snow to reflect what little light there is or define the line between open country, a river or a runway and the adjoining brush or trees.

Robin and Glenn went to town early enough to be prompt for the meeting. No one else went as they had to leave before the store was closed. The crew at the hospital was having a community picnic that evening and everyone was invited. The FAA had begun closing the station at night and all radio calls to the airport were transferred to Fairbanks.

The young fellow on duty that night finished his required shift, closed up the station as was normal and put the system on remote to Fairbanks—but he did not turn on the runway lights. They were not necessary earlier in the season. Naturally, when he went off shift there was plenty of daylight but it was after ten o'clock when Glenn and Robin returned and it was quite dark. The weather was still not bad but the overcast had increased until it allowed no stars to show through.

I was not at the picnic but a friend of ours told us later that everyone was wondering what that airplane was doing, why didn't he just land? Glenn finally flew down the river bank until he knew exactly where he was in relation to the runway, then swung over to meet the end of the runway but stayed low enough that his own landing light could illuminate the ground. He fishtailed, or swung the airplane heading back and forth, thus allowing the landing light to sweep back and forth over the ground. When he spotted the runway there was nothing to it. I'm sure I would have been much more nervous than I was had I known that he didn't have enough fuel left to go back to Manley Hot Springs, which also did not have runway lights. Suddenly that young communicator left the picnic, saying nothing, and ran down to the station and turned on the runway lights—after Glenn had made a successful landing! Barn door? Horse?

I think it is appropriate to point out that a pilot's wife didn't spend all her time sitting home by the radio or taking care of kids. After the younger children became responsible I often went with Glenn out to the Novi River cabin. Once we took a trip up the river in the boat as far above the cabin as we felt out gasoline would take us and leave a reserve for returning. We camped out on the point of a gravel bar where the wind would help keep the mosquitoes to a minimum. We set up our tent and were gathering firewood when I saw a bear coming directly for the tent. I shouted to Glenn and he hurried toward the tent where he had left his rifle. We just talked to the bear and explained to him that we only wanted to visit for one night and he went on by.

The next morning we started drifting down the river in the boat. As we drifted we tried to stay as near the middle of the river as we could but we could still hear the mosquitoes singing along the banks. Out in the river they were not bad. The scene was serene, quiet, and peaceful. The days were long and the weather was warm. We would stop at each likely looking gravel bar and search for nice looking agates. We also found some interesting ivory and mastodon teeth.

The last day, as we continued drifting toward the home cabin, we encountered a rainstorm that drenched the trees so heavily we could see water running right down the tree trunks. We could not see well enough to run the engine on the boat—beside that we had to bail steadily to stay afloat. About five miles above the cabin we saw a bear which was too close to our camp for comfort. He was digging little swallows out of their nests along the river bank. The Waite family, just across the river from us, needed the meat so we shot it and took it to them. They were very appreciative.

The twins went to Fairbanks for their last two years of high school. The thinking was that their dad was in town every week-day. If they were lonesome or really needed something, they only had to call his answering service for the flying business. In that way they were able to break away from home by degrees. When they went away to college it was not such a big move or abrupt break away. It seemed to work well. They handled it so well that I worried very little about the others as they matured and left home.

I think I spent much time waiting at home by the radio but not really worrying. I knew Glenn would come home eventually—he always had. However, now I feel more concern when he just goes up town, especially in the early fall or late spring when the roads are so icy. He really doesn't do a lot of driving but twice in the last few years a woman (a different woman each time), has pulled out in front of him at an intersection when he had the right of way. I was with him once.

To sum it all up, actually I think worrying is rather a waste of time. If it really did some good, fishermen and pilots' wives could surely put it to good use. It accomplishes nothing except to possibly add a few age wrinkles and I don't need them.

[1]HF—High Frequency
[2]VHF Very High Frequency
[3]LDS Church—The Church of Jesus Christ of Latter-day Saints

Epilogue

When Bud Conkle died, he held Master Guide's license #19 and had three Exclusive Guiding Areas assigned him by the Guide Licensing Board. His ashes are scattered over the airfield at Eagle Trail Ranch, and the tanned leather vest he was wearing when he died went with him. It was a trade mark with those who knew him. The bronze plaque from the American Legion, with his military record, is set in a rock that is permanently set near the windsock on the landing strip.

When Bud left us so suddenly there were many decisions I had to make. We had hunters booked two years in advance. I wrote to them to let them know and offered to refund their deposits, I gave them the choice of coming and hunting in the areas Bud would have taken them and they would have a dependable registered guide. Every one of those clients wrote back and said they had confidence in my ability to handle their hunt satisfactorily. It certainly boosted my confidence.

For two years I hired registered guides to take clients on the hunts they were booked for, then I sold or traded those exclusive guiding areas to younger guides who wanted to start out on their own. For the next ten years I lived at the ranch, taking tender loving care of the dependable furnace, and Lister generator for the needed electricity and a warm house. I sold the two Witte generators and bought a Lister that had an electric start. I had dependable neighbors I could call on if I had a problem. Ole Bates, living in Slana, kept my car running, generator repaired, and the water system drained when I was gone for some of the winter months, then activated it when I returned.

There comes a time in life when you realize it's time to move on. I enjoyed my life at the ranch and stayed as long as I felt equal to living there alone. I didn't feel alone because I had many friends who phoned or stopped, many pilots used the lake for landings, and always had time for pie and coffee.

I sold Eagle Trail Ranch in 1996 and bought a small home in North Pole next door to my son Colin and his family. My oldest son, Glen Huntley (from a previous marriage), came to help me move and get settled—he liked Alaska and stayed. Now with my two sons this close all the maintenance and any problems that may arise are taken care of. I have time to enjoy all the hobbies I wanted to do for so long—sewing projects and writing stories.